Four Evil Sisters

Esperanza Perez

Published by Trellis Publishing, 2021.

FOUR EVIL SISTERS

First edition. July 2, 2021.

ISBN: 979-8224443086

Written by Esperanza Perez.

FOUR EVIL SISTERS
ESPERANZA PEREZ

POQUIANCHIS: THE FOUR HORSEWOMEN OF THE APOCALYPSE

"They were evil!"

That was the title on the cover of January 1964 issue of Mexican magazine Alarma, which started media coverage of what would become one of the most infamous criminal cases in Mexican history. The story of the Gonzalez sisters had it all; kidnappings, prostitution, government corruption and mass murder.

EARLY YEARS

Carmen, Delfina, María de Jesús and Luisa Torres were born to Isidro Torres and Bernardina Valenzuela in El Salto, Jalisco between 1912 and 1936. Official documents show that Delfina was born in 1912, the exact year of birth of the three remaining sisters is uncertain.

Isidro conformed to the stereotype of a "Mexican Macho Man" of the early 1900s: alcoholic, violent and abusive towards his family. He worked as a "Juez de acordada," a law enforcement figure first instituted in Nueva España in 1736, in many ways similar to a Sheriff. The young sisters didn't receive any motherly love to offset the brutish nature of their father, Their mother, Bernardina, was a fanatical Catholic. She violently disciplined her children every time she judged their actions as sinful.

Like most serial killers, the Gonzalez sisters displayed warning signs at an early age. Carmen fled with a man many years her senior, something that was considered disgraceful by the societal standards of the time. But Isidro used his police contacts to find them and forced Carmen to return home. It was during this period that Isidro murdered a supposed criminal and was forced to become an outlaw. As a result, the girls had to drop the parental last name to evade problems with the authorities (Under Spanish naming customs the given name is followed by two family names. The first surname is the Father's first surname and the second the mother's first surname.) The sisters then became known as Carmen, Delfina, María de Jesús and Luisa Gonzalez.

Now free of paternal oppression the four sisters began dating older men; escaping the vigilance of their mother who had a rosary in one hand and a wooden paddle in the other.

THE SISTERS BEGIN AN ENTREPRENEURIAL CAREER

It was during the 1930s that the sisters found work in a textile factory working for peanuts. Working long hours and barely earning enough to eat was not an ideal state of affairs, so Carmen decided to launch a business venture. Investing the small inheritance they received after their parent's death, the sisters opened a second-rate tavern at El Salto that went bankrupt a few months later. This failure inspired Delfina to start a much more lucrative business, a brothel in El Salto's downtown. They financed the project with what Carmen was able to salvage from her failed enterprise. While the first months of this new establishment were a success, the operation had to be shut down in 1941 after a drunken quarrel ended up in a hail of bullets.

The industrious sisters quickly relocated their operation, if only temporarily, to San Juan de Los Lagos in Jalisco. They would target men who were visiting the nearby carnival and named their house of ill-repute "Guadalajara de Noche." Right after the end of the two-week carnival, Delfina with a lot of fresh cash decided to cross the state border and establish a new brothel in San Francisco del Rincón, Guanajuato. At this point, they struggled with the local authorities, since although not prohibited by law, brothels were considered to be against the best interests of the town. However, in Mexico, bureaucratic obstructions are easily removed with the proper motivation. City officials, police officers, and soldiers rapidly became, not only regulars to the "Guadalajara de Noche" (they decided to use the same name for this new brothel) but also providers of protection and security.

BUSINESS GROWTH 101

While running some errands in the state capital of León, María de Jesús met a former employee that she knew as Guadalupe Reinoso. Guadalupe had changed her named to "Laura Larraga" and was the head of one of the most exclusive brothels in the city. María de Jesús was impressed by the luxury and sophistication of Laura's establishment. She wondered how Laura could afford a house such as that; Laura told her she was leasing it from a gay ophthalmologist known in the scene as "El Poquianchis." María quickly realized that the success of Laura's business was not due to the tasteful interior design, but because the girls working there were very young and beautiful. Upon María´s return to the GDN´s headquarters, she sat in the war room with Delfina and told her about what she had seen in León. Both sisters decided that to reach the success they had always dreamt of it was necessary to improve the quality of their customer experience dramatically and relocate to a wealthier town.

The strategy was laid down; they required very young girls for the new place. To recruit them, Delfina traveled all around the "Bajio"(roughly translated as the Lowlands, a region in West North-Central Mexico formed by the states of Aguascalientes, Guanajuato, Jalisco, Querétaro and the neighboring state of San Luis Potosí.) During her journey, she talked to low-income families and promised the parents that she would take care of their teenage daughters and find jobs for them as housemaids in wealthy homes all over the state of Guanajuato (she coined the term "pupilas" or pupils to refer to the newly acquired employees.) They had enough savings to lease a house and set up shop in León, but money was not enough to start a new brothel in a big city; they needed local and public health permits. In the words of María de Jesús regarding her meeting with Mr. Fernando Liceaga, personal secretary to the mayor: << So he told me "why don't we go to your room so we can talk about the documents." I thought "he can issue me the permit right here, why does he want to go to my chamber?." I Understood what he was up to and well...I had to comply; we needed those permits. Once in the room, he said "I only want to be with you, to help, you know. You are getting those authorizations one way or another.">>

Regarding the public health permit, María de Jesús related her conversation with the then head of Municipal Public Health Dr. Castellanos <<"Look, honey. I will issue the permit, but you have to consider that we can no longer give them to new brothels, there is a limit, but if you become my little friend, we can do something about it.">>

Once the pressing issue with the permits was solved, María and Delfina had to negotiate terms with the local police department to make sure they wouldn't be bothered for employing mainly underage girls. The troopers needed a proper reason to turn a blind eye every time there was a violent altercation between customers; bribes were distributed not only amongst high ranking officials but to patrolmen as well.

LA CASA BLANCA

María de Jesús decided to call this new brothel "La Casa Blanca" (The White House). She then sent the pupils to hand out flyers all over the town. In spite of that, the attendance was meager at best. It is rumored, however, that the local priest and the sacristan showed up bearing bags filled with alms which they used to pay for the services of a few pupils.

Following the slow beginning of the new business venture in León. María Luisa, the youngest of the sisters, decided to gather her life savings (having worked as a cashier in all of the former brothels) and left in search of greener pastures in the coastal state of Veracruz. Delfina resolved to go on a second drafting tour all over the Bajio; she returned with a considerable number of young girls. This time, she chose to toughen the terms in which the pupils were working to ensure maximum profitability for the business.

EXPLOITATION AND TORMENT.

The recruits were put to work immediately, and because of the youth and beauty of the new girls, attendance skyrocketed in the space of a few weeks. In an attempt to profit from this situation, the sisters established a daily quota of services to be performed by every pupil. The practice produced many unwanted pregnancies. To save money, Delfina decided to take care of them herself, performing abortions on the teenage girls, with little to no regard to the necessary hygienic procedures required to ensure the well-being of the patient. As expected, this resulted in the death of a substantial number of pupils. The smartest of the pregnant pupils who succeeded in keeping their pregnancies a secret until childbirth had no better outcomes, as soon as the babies were born, they were taken and murdered by Delfina's lover.

The pupils were not only sexually exploited, but they also had to purchase their food, clothing, and supplies directly from Carmen and the sisters at inflated prices with substantial interest rates. This practice kept the girls in debt indefinitely. At least that was the plan, until 1949 when Carmen died from hepatic cancer. Considering that the other siblings couldn't read, let alone do some basic accounting, Delfina decided to forgive their debts in exchange for prayers to the soul of her deceased older sister.

EL POQUIANCHIS

A few weeks after Carmen's passing, María de Jesús received a surprise visit; it was no other than the notable Dr. Escalante (known as El Poquianchis), the gay ophthalmologist who owned the property where Laura Larraga's brothel was established. Laura's operation was in trouble and she was months behind on the rent. Dr. Escalante was now willing to sell to the highest bidder. and María de Jesús seized the opportunity. She bought the property for 25,000 pesos, thus expanding the sister's brothel operation in León.

The new brothel received the name "La Barca de Oro" (The Golden Vessel), but the regulars continued calling it "El bar poquianchis." María Jesús was to be commonly known as "La poquianchis," and after the scandal was made public by the magazine Alarma, the four sisters became recognized as "Las poquianchis."

PROSTITUTION AND RELIGION, HAND IN HAND

Even though the sisters were ruthless madams, they were first and foremost, zealous Catholics who considered there was nothing wrong with prostitution as long as some basic moral rules were strictly followed: Kissing, anal intercourse, lesbianism, and orgies were rigorously prohibited. The sisters took turns spying on the pupils while they were serving the customers to ensure there were no breaches of the code they enacted.

During her interview with journalist Elisa Robledo, María de Jesús revealed that sometime around the late 1950s, two American prostitutes arrived at the brothel and started working immediately. The new foreign pupils became an instant attraction, and customers waited in line for a chance to meet them. According to María de Jesús' account, they were caught in lesbian intercourse, expelled and allowed to return to the US. This way of dealing with the American girls seems to be contradictory since it was reported that whenever pupils broke the rules or were judged unfit for service, they were severely punished, deprived of food, bludgeoned, branded with hot irons and even murdered to be later buried in Delfina's nearby farm. In 1964, a grim discovery of over ninety bodies would be found in the farm.

The religious principles followed by the sisters also instructed against directly murdering the pupils, since murder is a deadly sin. According to Public Security Investigator Juan Pablo Arango, Delfina and María de Jesús never killed with their own hands. Instead, they employed mainly four male enforcers who were in charge of murdering and disposing of the bodies. The crew consisted of head enforcer (who was also Delfina's lover) former military officer Hermenegildo Zuñiga Maldonado, Valenciano Tadeo, Jese Lopez Alfaro, and Delfina's son, Ramon Torres a.k.a. "El Tepocate." Ramon suffered from Syphilis since his early teens which he got from one of the pupils.

The enforcers' primary job was to keep the pupils in check and to dispose of those that were judged unfit to keep producing for the company. María de Jesús and Delfina decided it was inconvenient to let pupils retire in peace since they could turn to the authorities and bring the whole operation down. The standard procedure was to have them murdered and buried in their farm, the infamous Rancho San Ángel in San Francisco del Rincón. Hermenegildo was also in charge of unburying the bodies after a few months, instructed to burn the remains and make them disappear; this practice has led to speculation that the actual victim count could have raised to more than 150 women (although supposedly only 90 bodies were found at the farm).

THE DOWNFALL

In 1962, elections were held in the state of Guanajuato and a new governor and mayor to the city of León were appointed. The sister's attempts to bribe the new administration, under Governor José Torres Landa, were unsuccessful. The recently elected officials decided to retaliate against the bribing efforts by enacting a new law that prohibited the operation of brothels in all the state of Guanajuato.

It is said that misfortunes come in threes, and this proved to be right for the sisters. A few weeks after having their operation shut down in Guanajuato, Delfina's son El Tepocate got involved in a quarrel with a federal agent at a bar where he was shot and killed. Seeking revenge, Delfina shot up the bar with her own rifle. She then proceeded to dress for mourning and instructed every pupil to do the same.

The whole company was forced into hiding at "Guadalajara de Noche" to avoid further problems with the law. The police forces, nonetheless, were made aware of Delfina's actions and soon arrived at the establishment. The sisters decided to lock themselves and the pupils inside the brothel, while the cops were instructed to stay and wait until the women attempted to leave the building.

After a few weeks, two of the pupils were sent to buy groceries from the local market where they were immediately apprehended. Delfina and the rest of the pupils took advantage of the ensuing confusion and fled through the back door. María de Jesús and the pupils headed straight back to Rancho San Ángel in San Francisco del Rincón, while

Delfina hurried to the city of Guadalajara in the hopes of finding a lawyer to take their case.

María de Jesús and the pupils had to remain in hiding for six months, while Delfina was distributing cash to government officials, cops and judges to avoid prosecution. Delfina's efforts would prove to be a complete failure. She then decided to join her sister at Granja San Ángel. It was during this mandatory ostracism forced on the pupils that some of them turned to desperate actions. A pupil caught a terrible infection after having intimate relations with a stray dog. Delfina had her killed after she found out about the pupil's sinful habits. The magazine Alarma later twisted this event; they claimed that bestiality was required from the pupils to satisfy the most exclusive clientele, which is almost certainly not true. Many more pupils died during this eight-month period due to the food shortages and precarious living conditions they had to endure.

After many unsuccessful attempts, pupil Catalina Ortega managed to escape from the brothel on January 12, 1964. Finally free from the sisters she rushed to the nearest police station where she disclosed where the sisters were hiding with the pupils. Captain Miguel Ángel Mota assembled a squad to raid the farm and arrest the sisters. María de Jesús later accused Captain Mota of being a hypocrite, as according to her statement he was a regular at La Casa Blanca. The accounts of many pupils later confirmed this claim.

An interview with former pupil Venenciana Marquecho Zamarripa appeared in the regional newspaper El Sol de San Luis in its February 6th, 1964 issue. In this interview, Venencia related her experience:

"My mother worked selling fruits at the park; I used to go there with her every day. One day she met Delfina who was on a "business trip" in the city. She offered to buy me; my mother was impoverished, so Delfina talked her into letting me go with her in exchange for 10 pesos. Delfina promised that she would find a decent and well-paid job for me in León, Guadalajara or Mexico City. I was only nine or ten years old. I recall they took me to Guadalajara, León, Lagos de Moreno, San Francisco del Rincón, and Querétaro. In all these places they forced me to sleep with older men, one time I didn't comply, so Delfina branded my face with a hot iron. Whenever one of the girls got pregnant or had a child, María forced abortions on them or killed the babies once they were born. One of the other girls told me that they used to make tamales out of the babies' remains and then served them to the customers in the brothels. My nightmare ended when they sold me for 500.00 pesos to a madam in Mexico City, and I managed to escape."

APPREHENSION AND DEATH

During the raid, María de Jesús and Delfina were apprehended together with the male enforcers, and two children between five and seven years old. The identity of these two boys is still a mystery to this day. The sisters were taken to the precinct in León and investigations were conducted on the farm. According to the reports, at least ninety bodies were found, along with a significant number of fetuses and unidentified human bones. The sisters denied any knowledge or involvement in the murders. Attorney Samuel Cruz declared in an interview to journalist Elisa Robledo: "No, there were never 90 bodies there were at most three, the official files and photographs show that no more than three bodies were recovered at the farm. The press and the authorities were against the sisters, so they turned to all this false information."

The sisters and their enforcers were then sent to the municipal jail in Irapuato, Guanajuato where they were to follow their process in pretrial detention. They almost didn't even make it to the prison, after an angry mob tried to lynch them outside the León precinct. Only a timely intervention by the police and military saved their lives.

The pupils declared the atrocities they had to endure during the time under the sister's care, giving the prosecutor a solid case. The youngest of the sisters, María Luisa, now comfortably living as a law-abiding citizen in the lush state of Veracruz, traveled to Guanajuato to support her siblings during the trial. However, upon arrival, she was charged and put into custody, although she had left the enterprise many years before. The prosecution accused her of satanic rites and witchcraft after finding amulets in her underwear; the press also exploited this event. Journalists claimed that the sisters held black masses and forced the pupils to perform satanic rituals. The sisters and their enforcers were sentenced to serve forty years under charges of kidnapping, conspiracy, human trafficking, child abuse, soliciting, murder, and illegal inhumation.

Delfina died in jail in 1968 after an accident when a crew of masons working on her cell accidentally dropped a bucket full of mortar fracturing her skull. María de Jesús was released from captivity in the middle of the seventies after her case was reopened; the court ruled that the investigation process was flawed. Upon release, María disappeared and would never be heard from again. Carmen died in 1949 of hepatic cancer, María Luisa died in 1984 of natural causes.

AFTERMATH

When the case was first disclosed in 1964 by the Mexican magazine Alarma, it became an immediate national sensation. The then recently created publication managed to sell more than two million copies of the magazine while the case was being covered. Today, with much more information available, it has become clear that the accounts were greatly exaggerated while details, stories, and testimonies were fabricated in an attempt to make the case viral.

There are a good number of books, movies, tv-shows, and documentaries about the case. Unfortunately, most of these are fictional works with very little to no accuracy in depicting the real facts. There are a few exceptions with one being the 1976 movie called "Las Poquianchis" directed by Felipe Cazals. While not a hundred percent accurate depiction of the facts, there are some truthful scenes.

CONCLUSION.

These events sent shockwaves all over Mexican society of the time, and reporters from at least five foreign countries were covering the case once it became famous. There is an undeniable desire to follow this kind of cases in every society. The Black Metal Murders in Norway, the monster of Florence in Italy or the Zodiac killer in the States, to name a few. Consumers are eager to follow these tales of murder and violence closely; while the press is always ready to seize the opportunity and twist the facts to make them sellable for as long as possible.

The tale of the evil sisters from El Salto was first reported by the then newly founded magazine Alarma, which recently ceased operations in 2014. The magazine became an icon of Mexican popular culture for more than forty years due in part to the savvy coverage of this particular case and its creative style of reporting the news. The story of "Las Poquianchis" not only offered a peek into the twisted minds of selfish murderers willing to do everything to keep their business thriving. It also disclosed the inner workings of a corrupt government and found deep faults in a society that on the cover was conservative, moralistic and religious.

cult of santa muerte

ANA BENSON

Silvia Meraz Moreno and the Cult of Santa Muerte

What is our picture of the perfect grandmother? Surely, they should be loving, spoilers of their grandchildren. Grandmothers should be a source of advice and support to their own children. Being a parent is a tough job, and the experience and skills that the older generation can offer can be a life-saver during the good times, let alone when things get tough.

But in the case of Silvia Meraz Moreno, we see a different side of the loving Grandma. Life taker is a better term to describe this grandmother than life saver. She led her family to slaughter her own grandson, sacrificing him to the altar of Santa Muerte, a bizarre and frightening cult whose base in Mexico is spreading, like some cankerous disease, to other parts of the world. In particular, to the United States.

Mexico is, of course, a strongly conservative and Catholic country. Religion might be playing an ever-decreasing role in the lives of its people, but for all that, it remains more influential than in most countries of the world. But Santa Muerte, despite the sound of its name with its suggestion of sainthood, is a cult that plays no part in the Catholic Church.

Indeed, the Church's leaders work hard to lessen the attraction of this strange and frightening cult, attempting to educate the poor members of society who are drawn to it. At the moment, they are not doing a very effective job

Santa Muerte is known by many names – Holy Death, Flaquita, which translates with a dark irony to 'skinny girl', or even Huesuda, or Bony Lady. For Santa Muerte is presented as a skeleton. A fleshless body often dressed in a white shroud, one whose presence is slowly, and disturbingly moving out of the dark recesses of private homes into mainstream life.

Effigies of 'Saint Death' now appear on the streets and market places of the most deprived, dangerous parts of Mexico. This trend began following the erection of a statue of the 'saint' on the sidewalk outside the home of Enriqueta Romero in the crime ridden Barrio of Tepito, one of the most impoverished parts of Mexico City. Pilgrims flock in their hundreds to offer gifts to the skeleton, which is bedecked in bright gowns and long, disturbing, hair. A moment's prayer, and the devotees are moved on to ensure the flow of people. Meanwhile, disinterested assistants spray holy water from a can onto the effigies the followers carry.

Fellow leader of the cult, Enriqueta Vargas has a seventy-five-foot fibreglass statue of Santa Muerte in her 'temple' in Tultitlan, where she conducts baptisms and weddings. The Skeleton Saint has even appeared on the television series, Breaking Bad and it is believed that there are upwards of two million followers of this angel of death in Mexico, and perhaps as many as six times that figure worldwide.

The cult that has grown up around this figure has taken on quasi-religious connotations. People, mostly young, offer sacrifices to the skeleton, and in return believe that she will grant wishes. Those sacrifices are typically the treats of the poor – cigarettes, sometimes food, alcohol along with fruit and flowers. She is inclusive in the granting of her gifts, treating the poor in the same way as the rich.

And, in a country where the poor and marginalised feel judged and out of touch with the Catholic Church, she is seen as one who will not judge the poor because of their circumstances, who values everybody irrespective of their background and wealth. It is a powerful message to hold in a country of such extremes of living standards as Mexico.

The 'religious' side of Santa Muerte's following has developed from the Catholic practices under which many of her devotees grew up. Rosaries, prayers and candles feature heavily in prayer to her, and physically, she bears an unmistakable similarity to the Virgin of Guadeloupe. In fact, her roots are not clear. Many believe that she rose from a combination of the practices of Spanish Catholicism, and the legends surrounding Mictecacihatl, the queen of the afterlife and underworld worshipped by the Aztecs.

Nowadays, she is the queen of the downtrodden, the marginalised, the criminals and the organised drugs cartels that are far too prevalent in many parts of the troubled country of Mexico. Prisons are crowded with her devotees. These people feel that they can ask for the granting of any favour, from better health through to protection from drugs trafficking, and as long as they pray, show gratitude and make an offering such wishes will be granted. Her attraction, though, is not limited to just the poor – to the dismay of the Catholic Church, she is attracting ever more followers from middle class homes.

But for all this, what she has not attracted, at least to the latter part of the first decade of this century, are human offerings.

It seems as though her cult originated in the Gulf or Mexico area, before taking a hold in Tepito and spreading from there to the barren border towns of Sonora, then north into the US and south towards Central America. Candles and prayer cards, along with other paraphernalia of Catholic religion, such as figurines, can be found in New York, Los Angeles and Chicago. For a short spell, the Cult of Santa Muerte was even recognised as an official religion in Mexico, but the authorities retracted the status after a couple of years.

Growth of cults such as Santa Muerte are not uncommon in Mexico, which has long had a tradition of worship for local folk heroes as well as devotion to Afro-Cuban and Aztec customs. But few, if any, have had the impact of this particular one.

Yet for a belief system so associated with the underworld of Mexican society, there has been little crime associated directly with the 'saint'. A bishop in the belief system was arrested for corruption in 2011, along with some of his congregation, although his supporters believe that he could well have been framed to bring a bad name to the cult and further disadvantage the downtrodden. David Romo was the bishop of a bright, many might say tasteless, shrine in the dangerous area of Tepito in Mexico City. Of course, the term 'bishop' is something of a misnomer. Any official status was self-appointed, because an organisation that is not officially recognised, and is not allowed to raise money or own property cannot, by definition, hold accredited positions in its hierarchy.

Romo was accused of money laundering and kidnap. The authorities claimed that he led a team of assistants (four men and three women were arrested at the same time as Romo) who collected ransoms through their bank accounts. Romo would organise the kidnaps, the ransoms would be paid to the 'assistants', who would take a small cut of the fee, and the rest would go to the bishop. Although he paid the kidnappers a small amount from that income, he was still making around 25000 pesos, which equates to about $1800, per kidnap.

Members of the Santa Muerte community are split on his guilt. Most feel that he is simply another easy victim of authorities seeking to discredit their cult. Others, though, suspect that the accusations might be true. They dismiss Romo and his followers as disloyal to the cult, people interested only in profit rather that true supporters of the unofficial saint.

But if it is true that the authorities simply framed him to discredit the cult of Santa Muerte, those in authority need only to have waited a little longer, because in 2012 the case of Silvia Meraz Moreno brought infamy to the cause, and all the publicity both the cult's followers, and its opponents, desired.

The State of Sonora in North West Mexico is a barren area, dominated by a mixture of the hot, dusty desert and crumbling mountains. Within that, there are touches of beauty; some of the beaches on the Gulf of California Coast are wonderful, and attract visitors from around the world. Silvia Meraz was born in the region's capital, Hermosillo, in 1968. It is a relatively wealthy city, liberal by Catholic Mexican standards, although even today gay and lesbian couples will attract stares or mistrust, although rarely outright opposition.

But mostly it is a friendly place, where visitors are welcomed, and the majority of the region's population can be found. We know very little of Silvia Meraz's background, but it appears as though education was minimal, and her upbringing was tough. This hard upbringing no doubt contributed to the strength of will that would later lead her to convince her family to participate in the vilest of acts.

At some point, she moved to Nacozari de Garcia, a small town close to Hermosilla, but a little to the north. This town existed on its copper mining. Meraz was already a grandmother by the age of 34, the father of her children certainly not on the scene, even if he were known. It is thought that Meraz ran a brothel, although the authorities were not that concerned about the matter.

In fact, the local community held Meraz's household in some sympathy. They were clearly very poor, had no obvious means of income and lived quietly on the edge of town in a crumbling shack of a home. There were only a couple of unusual events that caused some twinges of concern among the people of the town. Firstly, the number of strangers who seemed to visit – that was the basis of the authority's feelings that the home was a base of prostitution. Secondly, Meraz was the local leader of the cult of Santa Muerte.

People come and go in this part of Mexico. It is very rural, and extremely impoverished. While the nearby State capital is more liberal and cosmopolitan, the small town of Nacozari de Garcia liked to keep to itself.

So even when a ten-year-old boy disappeared, the investigations were cursory. Martin Rios disappeared in July 2010. The police spoke to the boy's mother, and also to her boyfriend, but they seemed unconcerned. Friends had reported that Martin had been seen in the town of Agua Prieta, a bigger community on the border with the US, close to the town of Douglas, Arizona. He had been begging there.

The daughter and the boyfriend promised to go and collect him, and the police were satisfied, and investigations ended. How the boy covered the 150 miles from Nacozari de Garcia to Agua Prieta, and who was tending for him in the bigger city were questions that were either not asked, or the responses were not fully investigated. No more was heard of Martin Rios for another two years.

Then, twelve months or so later, another ten-year-old went missing. Jesus Octavia Martinez Yanez was the grandson of Silvia Meraz. Local people noted that Martin Rios had been a regular visitor to the home of Meraz. Less surprisingly, of course, so was Jesus. Suspicions began to raise their heads. But there was no evidence for any wrong doing, just a vague feeling that things with the Meraz family were not all that they should be.

Searches in the locality led to no sign of the boy, nor any witnesses to his disappearance. Had he too left the small copper mining community to stay with friends or relatives, or on the streets, in a larger town? Was he begging on some street corner, vulnerable and alone? Or worse, had he been forced into the drugs trade – youngsters were often used as carriers and messengers, they were less suspicious than adults, many of whom would already be well known to police. Perhaps he too had been forced into prostitution, or the human trafficking trade.

A year after the disappearance of young Jesus, the link with Martin Rios was made, but still the Meraz family were not under suspicion. Certainly, it was known that that not only Silvia, the family matriarch, was a local leader for the Santa Muerte cult, but that her son was also heavily involved in the underground 'religion'. Yet, as we saw earlier, although many involved in the drugs trade followed the teachings of Santa Muerte, they had been no violent crimes directly tied to the belief system. There was no reason to suspect that the Meraz clan were responsible for a first.

Back in the 1980s, fifteen bodies had been discovered in Mexico, apparently slain in ritual killings. However, although suspicions had been present that there could be a link to the 'Holy Death' cult, it had seemed more likely that it was a drug's fuelled slaughter. The defence had claimed that the killers believed that by sacrificing the dead, which included 21-year-old American student Mark Kilroy, they would be protected from arrest. But no direct link between the slaughter and the Santa Muerte cult was proved.

Therefore, there was no particular reason to associate the family of Meraz with the disappearance of either of the young boys. However, the question of prostitution remained. Many in the town were convinced that this was going on at the house, but lack of evidence (and, probably, resources and time) had prevented any investigation. This, after all, was a town with a major drugs problem, where cartels were omnipresent, and where poverty presented plenty of problems of its own to the local law enforcers.

But now the authorities had an opportunity to investigate. The disappearance of the boys gave them a legitimate reason to search the collection of outbuildings and shacks where the Meraz family lived. Investigators felt that there was little or no probability of finding any evidence of the boys, but they expected to find evidence of other, less nefarious, activities.

But what they did discover shocked even the hardened investigators of the Mexican police.

One of the barns had been turned into a kind of place of worship, complete with altar. To their surprise, and horror, polices found evidence of blood spread for thirty square metres around that altar. Maybe it was ignorance on the part of Meraz and her followers, but it seems as though little effort was made to hide the blood. Perhaps the family believed that the Santa Muerte would protect them from prosecution.

Even then, police wondered more about the traces of blood. The area is notorious for violent crime, most of it emanating from the drugs cartels. But it was soon established that in this case, the perpetrators seemed likely to be based closer to home.

Although the Santa Muerte cult was growing fast, in the tiny town of Nacozari such interest as there was stayed close to home. Indeed, close to the family of Silvia Meraz Moreno. Then a breakthrough occurred. Police dug up the bedroom floor of one of Silvia Meraz's daughters, and there discovered the remains of Jesus.

With there seeming to be no other probable perpetrators of whatever crime had occurred, the police arrested the cult members. Along with Silvia, her partner Eduardo Sanchez, was taken into custody, and a link was soon found to the missing Martin Rios. It turned out that Sanchez had once been in a relationship with the boy's mother, Zoyla Hada Santacruz Iriqui, who was also arrested, and was later found to have agreed to her son's sacrifice. Silvia's three daughters were also arrested – Francisca Magdelana, the eldest at twenty-five, twenty-one-year-old Georgina Guadeloupe and Silvia Yahaira, who at fifteen is a minor under Mexican law, and would not be able to face trial until she turned eighteen.

Munro Palacio, an investigator in the case reported the disturbing news that the fifteen-year-old 'sees the religious practices of the family as normal.'

Others arrested were Meraz's son, Ramon Omar Palacios Meraz, and the grandmother's father, Cipriano Meraz Aguayo who was 83 at the time. But police were very clear that it was Silvia who was both leader and driving force behind this particular branch, a family branch, of the Santa Muerte devotees.

Once in custody, any sense that the family had prepared for discovery disappeared. Almost immediately. Discrepancies emerged between their stories. The police realised that they had on their hands a serious criminal event. Back at the Meraz's home they continued to search, and soon discovered that their gruesome discoveries were not over.

Cleotilde Romero was a 55-year-old woman, who had been a friend of the Meraz family. She had been reported missing back in 2009, but nothing had been found of her, until now. The extent to which the police searched for her at the time is difficult to say. A poor, marginalised woman in rural, poverty hit Mexico? The police would have had other problems which demanded their time. Her body too was discovered roughly buried in the vicinity of the home.

But it was not just that these three people, two of them young boys, had been murdered, it was the manner of their deaths that caused the greatest distress. It was clear that their demise had been ritualised. Slashes and cuts covered their bodies. It was soon obvious that the wide spread of the blood around the altar had been a result of the nature of their deaths.

The fear and horror that faced these victims is impossible to imagine, the pain would have been devastating. And two of the victims had been young children. In fact, Jesus Martinez had been virtually decapitated. It suggested a frenzy of violence, with no regard to the suffering it was causing.

As for those held in custody an entire raft of crimes was laid at their feet: first degree homicide, corrupting minors, illegal burial, robbery and conspiracy.

A spokesman for the prosecutors in Sonora state put the scale of the crimes into perspective. Jose Larrinaga said: 'They sliced open the victims' veins and, while they were still alive, they waited for them to bleed to death and collected the blood in a container.'

He went on to explain that the killings had taken place late in the evening, in a candle lit ceremony. Silvia Meraz herself had fallen into a delirious state, either genuine, or manufactured to influence the others involved.

'We all agreed to do it. Supposedly she (Cleotilde Romero) was a witch of something,' she said later. She would not comment on the deaths of the children.

Jose Larrinaga continued in his explanation of the ritual which saw the death of the three victims. He said that once the victims' blood had been collected, it was poured around the altar, and smeared into it.

The reason behind the murders was that Silvia believed that such a sacrifice would earn the family the favours of Santa Muerte. That she would act benignly on the family, and bring riches to them. She would take them out of the poverty of their lives.

It needs to be remembered that by the time of the killing, the cult of Santa Muerte had lost its briefly held official recognition in Catholic Mexico. In Nueva Loredo, a beautiful but crime ridden city to the east of the country, city workers had bull-dozed the many shrines to the false saint. But attempts to banish the cult from the country were not succeeding. Believers claimed that they had received all kinds of benefits from the skeleton deity. One convicted murderer told journalists that she protected the various items of contraband he kept in his cell by shielding them from the authorities. Presumably, following telling his tale, that shielding was short lived.

It is easy to see why a poor, disadvantaged family in a small copper mining town in northern Mexico might seek the support of anything that could help them out of their dismal existences. But to place riches above lives demonstrates a moral shallowness that cannot be defended.

When those lives are of a friend, as in Clotilde, and two young children, any lingering sympathy dissolves to nothing. Then, on top of this, we know that these children are, were, the sons and grandson of members of the sect.

Back in 2012, the State President of Sonora expressed his sadness that the power or Santa Muerte had led to these events in his region. 'As far as we know there are no more perpetrators,' he said, 'but we will see what information these people (the accused) provide, but the important thing is that they are already detained, and we will look to the full weight of the law to go against it.'

Following her arrest, Meraz appeared before the cameras with her daughters. Looking worried and deeply downcast, nevertheless she held true to her belief in Santa Muerte, holding a poster celebrating the saint of death.

And so, what can we conclude of this woman? It is hard to be sure of the state of her mind, as she sits in her prison cell, where she will remain for the rest of her life.

It is difficult to find much to say in her defence. It is probably the case that in her deluded state she did believe that a sacrifice to the 'white lady', as she is sometimes called, would help the family, offering them protection, wealth and health. It is also seemingly the case that during the sacrifices she did lose reason, hacking at the still living bodies with an axe and knives. It is certainly the case that the family lived in absolute poverty, and that most probably Silvia had been the victim of abuse herself. Perhaps she had been a prostitute, and had grown up without the guidance and support of her family which might have enabled her to develop a moral framework.

But we continue to come back to the horrific nature of her crimes, and that she dragged her own children into them. This was a family with a severely dark side.

And perhaps it is that which gives us the best insight into the actions of Silvia Meraz. This is a woman who is mentally unstable, who lacks any kind of empathy with others – it seems more than likely that she employed her own daughters in prostitution. In the end, the authorities ceased to pursue this investigation at the Meraz home, because the crimes they discovered where so much more insidious, but we know that it was widely believed the house was used as a brothel.

We also know that her fifteen-year-old daughter believed the kind of worship the family pursued was the norm. She had been infiltrated into the belief system so fully that she was able to participate in the murder of her own nephew. Therefore, we can deduce that the practices followed by the Meraz family were well established.

Although Santa Muerte seems not to have induced many killings and abuses directly – despite the fact that many of the followers of the cult have committed serious crimes in other circumstances – many other types of cults have. Unstable, sociopathic people are drawn to such organisations, and often rise to the top of them. In a situation where their behaviour is unchecked, they flourish. We have seen this in large scale events, such as the mass suicide of Jim Jones' cult in Guyana, and we see it on a smaller scale in abuses carried out in the name of satanic rituals.

Silvia Meraz Moreno was such a woman. Her individual sect was small, consisting of just her family. Who knows, had she lived in a larger community perhaps her individual branch of the cult of Santa Muerte would have been much bigger, attracting followers from outside her family. Perhaps in those circumstances, where she would no longer be the matriarch, others with less demonic moods might have tempered the actions of the cult, with sacrifices being no more than flowers, fruit and candy.

In that case, three people, including two young boys, would be alive, and eight others would not be sitting in prison.

But that was not how things turned out for Silvia Meraz. Poverty, an unsatisfactory upbringing, and a failure in the Catholic church to understand the extent of the impoverishment facing the underclass in Mexico were the factors in her life that could have been different. Living in a small community, where crime was rampant through the drugs cartels, added to the recipe that would lead to death. A different home town might have attracted the authority's attention to what was happening in the Meraz household, and the extent of the crimes committed there might have been limited to running a brothel or hosting prostitution.

We do not know if she enjoyed killing, if she felt remorse or if it was the failure of Santa Muerte to deliver the benefits she sought that drove her on to kill children.

But whatever, the crime is inexcusable. There are few who will argue that Silvia Meraz did not get exactly what she deserved.

SARA ALDRETE AND THE SERIAL KILLERS OF DEVIL'S RANCH

27

AARON GRIFFIN

EARLY LIFE

Sara Aldrete was born on September 6, 1964 in Matamoros, Tamaulipas, Mexico. As a teen, Sara was allowed to cross the border and attend Porter High School in Brownsville, Texas while her father supported the family working as an electrician. Teachers were fond of Sara as she was a well-behaved student who excelled academically. Her guidance counselor advised her to attend college immediately after graduation but Sara opted to marry instead. At the age of nineteen, she tied the knot with thirty-year old Miguel Zacharias on Halloween Day in 1983. The union did not last last, however, as they were separated and divorced within five months.

Two years later, Sara gained legal status as an American citizen. She enrolled at Texas Southmost College, a two-year school in Brownsville. She had been admitted on a work study program that minimized some of the tuition costs as she worked as both an aerobics teacher and assistant secretary in the school's athletic department.

Sara started classes in January of 1986 as a physical education major. At 6-feet-1 and with model good looks, she was a striking figure around campus.She became one of thirty-three students selected from over a 6,500 member student body to be included in the school's Who's Who directory for 1988. An active student on the campus, she organized a Booster club for the school's soccer squad as well as playing for the girl's volleyball team.

After the dissolution of her marriage, however, she had to move back home with her parents in Matamoros. They had constructed a patio/stairwell outside her second floor room so she could have some semblance of privacy. Sara came home on weekends and during the school breaks, hoping to transfer to a four-year program wherein she could receive a teaching certificate.

Her height and lithe physique caught the eye of many men, in particular Gilberto Sosa, a drug dealer who had ties with the powerful Hernandez family. She began dating Sosa while nurturing an interest in the religion of *Santería*. She learned about the religion's rituals and history during an anthropology class, immediately becoming obsessed. Ironically, this interest would coincide with meeting the man who would take her on a trip into darkness that she would never escape from.

"She would cross that border to Mexico," Lt George Gavito said. "And she would become somebody else."

GODFATHER AND GODMOTHER

Sara was driving through Matamoros on July 30th, 1987 when she nearly got into a car accident with a young man driving a luxury Mercedes-Benz. The young man got out of the car acting apolegetic. Sara was immediately taken by his good looks and well-spoken nature. His introduced himself as Adolfo Constanzo. They exchanged information and Adolfo expressed excitement when he learned that Sara shared the same birthday as his mother.

What Sara didn't know was that the near miss on the Matamoros street was carefully choreographed. Adolfo had been stalking Sara's boyfriend, Gilberto, assessing how much power he had in the drug dealing Hernandez organization.

Adolfo quickly befriended Sara and seduced her with his knowledge of the occult. In a subsequent meeting, Adolfo met the couple together, completely ignoring Gilberto's offer of a handshake and focusing his attention exclusively on Sara.

Later, an anonymous phone call informed Gilberto that Sara was dating someone else. The drug dealer went into a jealous rage and confronted Sara. She denied the allegations but he broke off the relationship anyway.

Sara then turned to Adolfo for comfort. He told her that he knew that Gilberto would break up with her as he had seen her future in a tarot card reading. Adolfo proceeded to "comfort" Sara by seducing her but their physical relationship would not last.

"Sara started dating Constanzo until she found out he was gay," Gavito said. "She said 'no problem'. But he told her what was he was involved in and she introduced him to the Hernandezes. So it was Sara that was the one that connected all of this people together."

Adolfo wanted a meeting with the leader of the Hernandez family, Elio, and Sara arranged for that to happen. Adolfo saw that he could influence drug dealers with his dark magic and earn a nice living for himself. Charming Elio Hernandez would be step one toward that goal.

When Sara returned to the college, her classmates noted that her demeanor changed significantly. Sara obsessed on witchcraft and magic in every conversation. She wanted to argue on the merits between good and evil.

Sara eventually left her studies behind and Adolfo welcomed her into his growing cult. He christened her as "La Madrina", the Godmother. He himself was "El Padrino", the Godfather.

WHO WAS ADOLFO CONSTANZO?

Adolfo was born in Miami, FL on November 1st, 1962 by a fifteen year old girl who would subsequently have three children by three different men. His mother, named Delia Aurora Gonzalez, had her son blessed by a Haitian priest who practiced *palo mayombe*, a form of witchcraft that owes its origins to the Congo but was passed down to Cuba and Puerto Rico with the settlement of slaves.

The boy's mother was excited when the Haitian priest pronounced that her six month old child was "chosen" and "destined for great power."

Delia moved the family to San Juan, Puerto Rico shortly after his baptism. Adolfo's childhood was steeped in the teachings of the dark imaginings of his mother. She taught him the rituals of her bizarre religion even as he became an altar boy at the local Catholic church.

When Adolfo was ten, his mother moved her growing family back to Miami. They once again met with the Haitian priest and young Adolfo began an apprenticeship under the man.

A MOTHER FROM HELL

Adolfo's mother Delia was arrested over thirty times. Her rap sheet included shoplifting, passing false checks, grand theft and child neglect. Her punishment, however, was always lenient and she was never sentenced to anything more than probation. She attributed her ability to escape jail stints to the spells she cast under *palo mayombe* and she passed down this belief system to her son.

A true tenant from hell, she left every apartment she stayed in a vandalized mess. Delia left the walls and floors bloodstained with the remains of animals that she sacrificed. Living in a section of Miami known as the Coral Park Estates, Delia lorded over her neighbors in a reign of terror. Earning her reputation as a witch, Delia was vindictive with anyone who dared inspire her wraith. Neighbor Elena Menendez found a dead goose on her door step with its head wrapped in a red handkerchief. Carmen Reiganda opened her door to find a decapitated chicken on her porch after her son had gotten into an argument with Delia.

Mother and son left a legacy of fear behind in the small Miami neighborhood and the majority of the people were afraid to talk about them.

"Everyone here is worried (Adolfo) will come back to get them for talking," said one man. "I've completely protected my house, and if they come by, I'll blow them away."

LIKE MOTHER, LIKE SON

Adolfo inherited both his mother's religion and criminal ways. He indulged in Miami's gay bars during his teens and earned a living through petty theft. He found school to be a burden and was only interested in learning about black magic. The boy barely graduated from high school and dropped out of junior college after one half-hearted semester.

He continued to obsess about witchcraft with his Haitian priest mentor. They formed a team to rob graves at midnight to stock the priest's lair with dead bodies. They created voodoo dolls and sprinkled blood over them to curse people that crossed them.

The philosophical tenets of *palo mayombe* laid the foundation for Constanzo's future drug dealing endeavors. The belief system places no value judgments on the individual, there is no "good" or "evil" magic. Criminals familiar with the practice used it to protect them from the law but the Haitian priest had a solemn warning for his young student.

"Let the non-believers kill themselves with drugs," the priest said. "We will profit from their foolishness."

By the age of fourteen, Delia became convinced that her son had psychic abilities. Adolfo claimed to have predicted that President Ronald Reagan would be shot by John Hinckley. Adolfo had a murky vision for his own future, however, as he was arrested twice for shoplifting in 1981, including one incident where he tried to steal a chainsaw.

Two years later in 1983, Adolfo had sworn his allegiance to *Kadiempembe*, the name for Satan in *palo mayombe*. The Haitian priest gave Adolfo his blessing as the boy vowed to worship evil in return for financial gain. The priest initiated Adolfo into the fold with a ritual scarring as he took a knife and sliced arcane symbols into the body of his young student.

"My soul is dead," Adolfo said at the end of the ceremony. "I have no God."

BEGINNING OF A CULT

Blessed with good looks, Adolfo landed a modeling gig in 1983. He traveled to Mexico City for a photo shoot and earned some extra money telling fortunes with tarot cards in the city's dangerous Zona

Rosa (Spanish for "Red Zone", a strip of prostitutes, bars and drug dealings.)

The trip to Mexico netted him his first cult followers which included Martin Quintana Rodriguez, Jorge Montes, and Omar Orea Ochoa. Adolfo had affairs with Quintana and Orea, wherein he would be the "woman" or the "man" in the relationship depending on his mood.

In 1984, Adolfo moved his base of operations to Mexico City permanently. He lived with both Quintana and Orea, engaging in nightly homosexual ménage à trois. He began offering his psychic services around the city, developing a reputation for seeing into the future and offering *limpias.* These were ceremonial "cleansings" for those who thought they were cursed by life or wanted some enemies taken care of.

Adolfo kept records of his dealings with the townfolk and his journals revealed that he had thirty-one regular customers. Some of his patrons would pay up to $4500 for one single ritual. Adolfo gave his customers a menu in which they had a choice of sacrificial animals to choose from. Roosters went for $6, goats $30, boa constrictors $450, zebras $1100, and African lion cubs were $3100.

Adolfo began to target the more successful drug dealers in the area. He would help them schedule shipments and customers based on his own alleged "visions". He would charge exorbitant fees for his "magic" to make dealers and their henchmen invisible to police and remain bulletproof against would-be assassins.

Most of the drug merchants had upbringings that paralleled Adolfo's in that their parents were poor peasants who believed in the supernatural. They made for easy dupes for the charismatic cult leader who had one dealer pay him over $40,000 for his supernatural blessings over a period of three years.

Adolfo always delivered, however, as he realized that at such prices his magic would have to be just that, a magic show spectacle. On one occasion he and three of his followers broke into a Mexico City graveyard and excavated numerous graves for bones. His reputation grew as his stage show became more elaborate. He was soon entertaining physicians, business men, fashion models and a host of transvestite cabaret singers. In a bizarre twist, there were several high-ranking police officials that joined Adolfo's cult. The most notable was Salvador Garcia Alarcon, a lead narcotic investigator and Florentino Ventura Gutierrez who was the head of the Mexican branch of Interpol.

The devotion of these individuals clearly went beyond mere bribery or charm. It soon became apparent that they worshiped the young Satanist as he led them on a tour to all of the pits of hell he could dream up.

A year later, Ventura would introduce Adolfo to the infamous Calzada family, arguably Mexico's biggest drug cartel at the time. Letting his charisma do the work for him, Adolfo won the gang over with an elaborate ritual and they repaid him for his blessings of "magic". By 1987, Adolfo had amassed enough cash for a luxury condo and a slew of high-end cars which included an $80,000 Mercedes-Benz.

"Constanzo made these people believers," Gavito said. "I think it could happen to anybody. Most of these kids came from good families. And they're already involved in moving narcotics. So I think it was easy to graduate into the cult part of it. Because they saw the wealth and they saw the power that Constanzo had."

Adolfo liked to push the envelope, however. Not satisfied with his payments from the drug dealers, he disguised himself as a DEA agent and relieved a Guadalajara dealer of his cocaine stash. He sold the coke through his police connections for a $100,000 profit.

As the stakes rose, so did Adolfo's need to have more over-the-top rituals. It was during this time that he began incorporating human sacrifice into his ceremonies. His callousness in both torturing strangers and his closest friends scared both the dealers and police officials into remaining on his good side if they could.

The Calzada drug cartel bought into Adolfo's act hook, line and sinker. The simple minded drug dealers attributed their continued prosperity and survival to his magical powers. Adolfo sensed his influence over the family and realized that he had became a necessary "good luck" charm to them. In the spring of 1987, Adolfo called for a meeting with the heads of the Calzada family. He demanded to become a full partner in their drug dealing enterprise.

The Calzada family rejected the notion immediately.

Adolfo, however, realized that if he was not going to be given power then he would take it.

On April 30th, 1987 Guillermo Calzada Sanchez and six members of his family disappeared under suspicious circumstances. They were reported missing on May 1st with the authorities discovering remnants of what looked like a Santería ceremony at Calzada's office as they found as melted candles and bones scattered about. A week later, mutilated remains washed ashore on the Zumpango River. The police trolled the river and recovered the seven bodies. All of the corpses showed signs of severe torture: fingers, toes and ears were removed, genitals slashed, a spinal column was excised from one body, two others had their skulls opened with their brains missing.

The body parts of the Calzada drug cartel were now part of Adolfo's growing *nganga* or cauldron, a large iron kettle where he stirred up his "witch brew."

His primary drug competitors now eliminated, Adolfo believed that he was growing stronger in his dark magic and began setting his sights on bigger targets.

The Hernandez family became next on his to do list. Adolfo set up a meeting with the powerful Elio Hernandez through Sara who had been dating his son. Adolfo had received word that the Hernandez cartel had dissension in the ranks and were becoming more vulnerable to competing drug families.

During their talk, Adolfo convinced Elio of the efficacy of the *palo mayombe*. He seduced him with the idea of taking his enemies and sacrificing them to his Satan God. In return, Adolfo promised that his family and drug enterprise would be blessed by the dark forces, that they would become invisible to police and bulletproof.

"Give me fifty percent of the profits," Adolfo said. "And I'll control things."

THE BELIEVERS

In 1987, Adolfo became obsessed with a film called the *The Believers* which starred Martin Sheen and Jimmy Smits. It was a movie that showcased the Santeria and voodoo possession and Adoflo saw himself in the characters. He sought to replicate what he saw on the screen into his own rituals.

"It is not at all surprising that Constanzo and Sara Aldrete were infatuated with the movie *The Believers*," said occult researcher Carl Raschke. "The magical practitioners in the film are portrayed as insuperable and almost all knowing."

Adolfo saw the film as validation for what he was doing, specifically conjuring up the spirit realm to aid him in his crimes. Sara, on the other hand, used the movie as a recruiting tool for prospective members.

"[There is]...a story making the rounds that tells of the night Aldrete persuaded three male friends to screen a video of *The Believers*," Rolling Stone magazine reported. "After the film, say the students, Aldrete stood up and began to preach in strange tones about the occult. 'They had been drinking and they just thought she was trying to be spooky,' said one of the students who knew the boys. 'but they look back on it now and think she must have been serious.'"

THEY MUST DIE SCREAMING

Adolfo's thirst for more power and wealth required that his rituals become more specific and gruesome. He moved his cult to a place called Rancho Santa Elena which was about twenty miles away from Sara's hometown of Matamoros.

On May 28th, 1988, Adolfo murdered a drug dealer named Hector de la Fuente and a farmer named Moises Castillo in sacrifices to his demon God. Not satisfied with the level of sadism he achieved in those killings, he then tortured and mutilated a transvestite named Raul Paz Esquivel. Paz was a former lover of one of Adolfo's original followers, Jorge Montes. The level of torture was extreme as they dismembered Paz's body, turning him into a bloodied pretzel. Paz' dismembered body was then left on a city street only to be discovered by school children.

Sadism and torture became foremost on Adolfo's mind as he sought new ways to increase his depravity. Invariably, he would sodomize his victims before their death, giving them one last indignity. Blood and guts fed his cauldron where Adolfo turned the "stew" like a modern day witch. He believed that the devil he worshiped would be more pleased if his sacrificial victims suffered as much as possible.

"They must die screaming," Adolfo intoned to his followers.

THINKING BIG

On August 10th, 1988, rival drug dealers kidnapped Ovidio Hernandez and his two year old boy. They wanted revenge for being ripped off on an $800k deal.

Adolfo, feeling the need to show off the efficacy of his *palo mayembe*, kidnapped a random stranger off the street and brought him to the ranch. They tortured the man, offering him as a sacrifice to their Satanic God while praying for the safe release of the Hernandez family member and his son.

Three days later, the dealers released Hernandez and the boy without any ransom money being exchanged. The Hernandez family gave full credit to Adolfo and his use of witchcraft.

He had them under his spell...

NO SAMPLES FOR YOU

Three months later, a 35-year old ex-policeman turned cult member named Jorge Valente de Fierro Gomez was caught using drugs, stealing from Adolfo's stash.

Adolfo decided to make an example out of his follower as he didn't want any of his members to partake in the drugs. The ex-cop became yet another sacrificial offering to *Kadiempembe*.

On Valentine's Day of 1989, Adolfo's group captured three competing drug dealers and tortured them to death. They dismembered the bodies and added them to the gruesome brew. A week later, another sacrificial victim had been kidnapped but the man put up such a lengthy fight that the group was forced to kill him before he could be tortured. The followers continued their quest to acquire victims. They came upon a 14-year old boy and killed him before realizing that the teen was a cousin of Elio Hernandez.

The boy cried uncontrollably as Adolfo's henchmen had the knife to his throat. Adolfo decided that the boy could be added to the brew because he was too sad. If they sacrificed the boy, then the demon god would be sad. So they killed the boy and went out to the streets to find another young boy.

Adolfo did this because he wanted to acquire the boy's youth. When he wanted "youth" he would have a young boy kidnapped and sacrificed. When he wanted "strength", he would have a strong man kidnapped and dismembered into his brew.

SPECIAL BLESSING NEEDED

By this time, Adolfo had amassed over 800 kg of marijuana that his followers had stolen from another gang. He thought he needed a special blessing to ship the large amount across the Rio Grande. His followers kidnapped another stranger off the streets but Adolfo was not satisfied with the level of sadism they had achieved in torturing the man. He felt that his demon overlord, *Kadiempembe*, would require a new benchmark in torture and pain.

"Bring me someone I can use," Adolfo said. "Someone who will scream."

He also wanted someone smart, someone who had medical training. He instructed his followers to keep their ears out and find an American college student who was going into the medical field.

The next morning, his followers brought in a young college student named Mark Kilroy.

SPRING BREAK HORROR

Matamoros had been a popular hangout for college students on spring break for decades. Students would come upon the small Mexican city looking to let loose in the uninhibited foreign soil that offered prostitution, nudie bars, booze and drugs.

By March of 1989, however, the town had over sixty unsolved disappearances over the course of three months. Unfortunately, this did not deter the usual contingent of American collegians from descending upon the town and enjoying the nightlife.

Mark Kilroy was one of those tourists.

A popular high school student, he played on the basketball and golf teams. He served on the student council and graduated 14th in a class of 210. He initially enrolled at Tarleton State on a basketball scholarship but transferred to the University of Texas after two years, giving up his basketball aspirations to concentrate on his pre-med courses. He was, by all accounts, an upstanding young man.

His father, Jim Kilroy, recalled that when his son was in high school, he would sometimes go to Mark's bedroom to make sure he was studying. He would find the young man reading his Bible instead. "What do you do?" Kilroy asked as he recalled the memory of his son. "He needs to study. But do you go in and tell your son to quit reading the Bible?"

Mark had trekked to Mexico for the spring break with three friends who were all his former classmates at Santa Fe High in Texas.

"The whole semester," a friend recalled. "That (the trip) was all we talked about."

They spent the night enjoying the Mexican food and drinking. They chatted with some girls visiting there from Kansas then returned without incident to their rooms at the Sheraton Hotel on South Padre Island over 20 miles away.

The second night would be quite different. They spent the evening drinking and then around 2 o'clock in the morning they began walking toward the bridge which connected Matamoros with the Texas border town where they had parked their car. Two of Mark's friends walked ahead while Mark and Bill Huddleston lingered about twenty feet behind. Huddleston briefly stepped into an alley to urinate. Mark waited on the street.

When Huddleston came back onto the street he could not find Mark anywhere. There were no signs or sounds of struggle.

THE ABDUCTION

Four of Adolfo's followers had kidnapped Mark. They had been driving a red pick up truck along the main drag of Matamoros, tailing the group unnoticed.

When they spotted Mark alone, they offered him a ride.

"They all had badges that said 'state police,'" Gavito said referring to the fact that Adolfo's followers disguised themselves as cops. "They all had jackets that said police on them. They had red lights in their car. They ran around Matamoros like they were police officers. When (Mark) went off to use the bathroom that was the perfect time. They went up to him, they badged him, they put him in a car, they told him he was under arrest for being drunk. They drive down about two blocks. They pull over, they all get out, the policemen, the guys 'acting' as policemen. They wait for the other car to show up. (Mark) jumps out and starts running."

Mark Kilroy ran for two blocks. The Constanzo crew chased him down yelling "freeze".

"(Mark) being the well educated boy that he is," Gavito said. "Who was brought up to respect the law, when he heard the word 'freeze', he stopped. He was half a block from getting back on the main drag where there was two thousand kids partying. And he stopped, they handcuffed him, they threw him back in the car, they took him back to the ranch. They tied him up and they put him in the back of the Suburban."

He was given food and told he would not be harmed.

Twelve hours later, however, he would be sacrificed.

Kilroy was the only American kidnapped by the cultists. He also came from an affluent family including an uncle that worked for the U.S. Customs Service. His father was a chemical engineer and his mother a volunteer paramedic. The family were devout Catholics, active in their local church.

The response from from the public was immediate. There was a $15,000 reward for information leading to his return or the arrest of his kidnappers.

Yellow bows graced the churches of his hometown and beyond. Dozens of people joined the search for Kilroy, with hundreds of flyers being handed out around the town. San Antonio Mayor Henry Cisneros lobbied Mexican authorities to find the young man.

"I had worked with the Mexican police for over twenty years," Lt. George Gravito recalled. "Best cooperation you've ever had in your life. All of a sudden, I ran into a wall. No cooperation. The state police was telling us that (Mark) was involved in narcotics. But they wouldn't tell me where they're getting the information. This guy was corrupt. What we're meeting with right here on the border, one day you're investigating a crime in Brownsville, Texas and tomorrow morning you're investigating it in Matamoros, Mexico. It's not your jurisdiction and you have to know how to move around. You can't step on the wrong toes because they're gonna kick you out of the country."

The Matamoros police interrogated over one hundred known criminals in the area in the search for Kilroy. They beat their legs with clubs and sprayed soda water mixed with hot sauce into their nostrils.

They came up with nothing.

ONE MORE SACRIFICE

Adolfo had used the sacrifice of Kilroy in his mind to ensure the safe shipment of his marijuana. But now, he thought he needed yet another special sacrifice to his palo mayombe overlord.

Adolfo decided to target Sara's former boyfriend, Gilberto Sosa.

On March 28th, 1989, Sosa became the cult's final sacrifice as the marijuana made its way across the Rio Grande on April 8th.

Adolfo's alleged psychic abilities would fail him, however, as his depraved empire would soon come to an end in a way that he didn't foresee...

PURE LUCK

The police drew no leads for two weeks until they came across a "happy accident" on April 10th of that year...

"We were lucky," Gravito recalled. "What helped us in this investigation was, we had been working on some narcotic cases. DEA Brownsville had been working real close with *un commandante* in Matamoros. That *commandante* was Juan Benitez Ayala. He was the head of the federal police assigned to the Matamoros area. This man, Juan Benitez Ayala, I'll say was about five feet tall. But he probably stood about eight foot tall. I mean when this guy walked in anywhere people were scared of him. He worked and that's all he did.

"You didn't see him in bars. You didn't see him in restaurants. And the reason he didn't go to bars or restaurants, one, he was afraid someone might put something in his drink and kill him. The guy was taking down some powerful people in Mexico and we went to talk to him."

"I told him we got this problem with this state police guy, he says these kids were involved in narcotics, and I assure you that they weren't. We had helped them on some cases, we had busted some big people (because) we had shared some information. So he put his people to work. And every time we had a lead, we'd call him, we'd go over there, we'd kick doors down, you know, you don't need a search warrant, the search warrant IS the federal police and nobody gets in your way."

The Mexican police had erected roadblocks and began a random drug roust in areas of Matamoros unrelated to the Kilroy disappearance. They had a policy of targeting only the low level runners and leave the heads of the drug operations alone.

Serafin Hernandez was the epitome of the low-level drug dealer. He was the twenty year old nephew of Elio Hernandez and a well known trafficker. During this drug roust, Serafin came across the police checkpoint and was followed. He unknowingly led the officers to the innocuous looking cattle ranch. A shabby looking corral marked the front with a tar paper and wood shack that stood in the rear of the winding, unmarked road.

It was Rancho Santa Elena, the home of Constanzo's cult.

The police waited a week and returned en masse, arresting both Serafin and another dealer named David Serna Valdez. The interrogations began and the two dealers proved to be cocky witnesses. They claimed they were "protected" by supernatural powers, of course referring to the spells that Adolfo had cast.

Inside, the police found a horror chamber beyond the imagination of any snuff film. The 15x25 foot shed was saturated with blood and smelled of rotting flesh. They found human brains, hair, teeth and skulls. Some spines had been crafted into necklaces. Scattered around were machetes and white votive candles in a box that bore a picture of *Our Lady of Guadalupe.*

The press nicknamed Rancho Santa Elena as the "Devil's Ranch."

"I thought in my twenty two years of law enforcement I had seen everything," a Texas deputy said. "I hadn't. As we drew near, you could smell the stench...blood and decomposing organs. In a big, cast iron pot there were pieces of human bodies and a goat's head with horns."

MAKING THE CONNECTION

"About two o'clock in the morning I get a call from *el commandante*," Gavito recalled. "We found (Mark) he said. 'You found (Mark)? You kidding?' he said no. We found (Mark). Where? He said he's buried in a ranch outside of Matamoros. I asked him how? Or who? He said there was a caretaker that also lived near the ranch. When he arrested Serafin, he picked him up too, the caretaker, but he didn't file charges against him. But he kept him under house arrest and the caretaker saw a picture of (Mark) on top of the table. And he pointed to it and said 'I know that boy'. 'How do you know him?' 'I was feeding him. I was giving him bread. I untied one of his arms so he could sit up and eat' because they had him tied to the back of a Suburban."

El Commandante then began interrogating Serafin. Without prompting, Serafin began offering information on how he knew Mark Kilroy, admitting that he was the one who kidnapped him.

"This guy was volunteering all of this information," Gavito said. "I mean usually in Mexico you have to go, you know, I guess its something you have to know when you get arrested, that they're going to torture you to get the truth out of you. But I've never heard of anybody just confessing this easily as Serafin. And we kinda talked a little bit and the name Constanzo had come up on his investigations. Serafin had said that they had kidnapped (Mark) because the *Padrino*, Constanzo, wanted somebody who was studying medicine because they were doing some kind of witchcraft."

"They were going to use Mark's brain to give it to this pot that they had. And I didn't understand what he was talking about and I said did you have to torture this guy and he said 'no, this guy (Serafin) thinks that bullets do him no harm and the police can't hurt him he thinks that this guy, this Constanzo is gonna come in here and take him out of here."

"It's our religion," Serafin said. "Our voodoo."

George Gavito recalled that during Serafin's confession he repeatedly made reference to the aforementioned film, *The Believers.*

"I remember I didn't understand what he was telling me," Gravito said. "I said, 'Is it Santeria?' And he said, 'Yeah, yeah, Santeria, voodoo, man.' And then he kept on saying, 'The Believers, The Believers, The Believers.'"

"Elio made [Serafin] Garcia a priest, but Garcia didn't really know what he was practicing because all he had on his mind was the movie."

Serafin told the authorities about El Padrino, the Godfather, as being Adolfo Constanzo. He revealed the details of Adolfo's ritual of African magic, palo mayombe. "Adolfo ordered the slayings," Serafin said. He revealed that the Godfather had tortured and sodomized his victims before killing them. They would then mutilate the bodies and harvest the organs for his witches brew.

SCENE OF THE CRIME

Serafin was brought back to the Devil's Ranch with Ayala and Gavito, both police officials not expecting the level of depravity they were about to investigate.

"We asked him where the body was," Gavito recalled. "And he said 'which body?' Just like that. 'Which body?' 'Man,' El Commandante says. 'Man, if you're playing games with me' and he got pissed off. And he (Serafin) says 'hold on, which body you want?'"

"'What do you mean, which body!'" El Commandante screamed.

"There's a bunch of bodies out here," Serafin said. "Which one do you want?"

"What do you mean?"

"Yeah," Serafin began walking through the corrals. "There's one buried here, there's one buried there."

"How many?"

"I don't know."

"Where's Mark?"

"Over there in the corner."

"Where?"

"I don't remember exactly," Serafin said as he started walking to a corner of the corral. "But I think it is where that wire is."

The police looked down and saw a coat hanger half-buried in the dirt.

"Why a coat hanger?"

"Oh, because Constanzo wanted to make a necklace," Serafin said. "With Mark's backbone. So after we killed them and everything we ran wire through his back, through the spinal cord, so that later on we could just come and get it out and he could make a necklace."

Disgusted and angry, Benitez-Ayala handed Serafin a shovel, forcing him to dig up the body of Mark.

During the dig, Serafain revealed that Constanzo had killed Mark with one machete slice to the back of his head. He began revealing more details of other killings, matter of factly and without feeling. At one point he even asked if the police we're going to order food because he was getting hungry.

El Commandante Benitez-Ayala became enraged. He took out his Uzi and fired the weapon into the air out of frustration.

"You don't think bullets can hurt you?" he asked Serafin.

"No," Serafin replied.

El Commandante then began emptying his entire clip.

"That's when the kid's eyes opened up," Gavito recalled, remembering how frightened Serafin became. "I mean his eyes opened up when he heard that sound, I mean it freaked us all out because we didn't realize what was going on. He (Serafin) went from being a believer to being a disbeliever pretty quick. He went back to being a normal person."

Serafin suddenly snapped out of his brainwashed state.

"I don't know why they got us to do this," Serafin said.

"All of a sudden it was 'why' they got us to do this," Gavito said. "It just changed."

His body unearthed, Kilroy's skull had been split open and his brain removed. The police then found a nearby shed wherein they located Adolfo's *nganga*, a cast-iron cauldron that was stained with blood, body parts and numerous sticks, the "palos" of *palo mayombe*.

Inside the kettle were spiders, scorpions and the brain of Kilroy. His brain had been boiled in blood over an open fire along with a turtle shell, a horseshoe, a spinal column and other human bones.

FAILING MAGICAL POWERS

Adolfo was surprised at the reaction to Kilroy's disappearance. He was used to his killings not gaining any notoriety at all. Even after the fact, three of the unearthed victims have never been identified and only a handful were reported missing.

The next day, all hell break loose for the cult members. Four members of the Hernandez family were arrested and the cash from their big marijuana sale was confiscated. The police began unearthing bodies from the ranch on April 11th, finding more bodies in a nearby orchard.

Feeling the heat, Adolfo went on the run with Sara, and his two lovers Martin and Omar. A Hernandez family hit man named Alvaro De Leon Valdez, nicknamed "El Duby", came along as well.

Adolfo's first instinct was to go to Miami where he could be with his mother. He decided to stay travel to Mexico City, however, using the homes of followers and friends of followers to hide.

The gruesome discoveries made the rounds in tabloid television. Geraldo Rivera produced a segment on the murders. There were false sightings of the cult being reported in the United States. Adolfo was claimed to have been seen in Chicago where people mistakenly labeled him as part of the Windy City Mafia. Sara was reportedly seen skulking around schools throughout various border towns, threatening to kidnap and kill ten white kids for every one of her followers that were jailed in Mexico. There was a church located in Pharr, Texas that was burned down after rumors that some if its members were connected to Adolfo's cult. Serafin Sr, a drug dealer and follower of Adolfo, was found and arrested.

The national news did little to shed light on the whereabouts of Adolfo, however. They successfully hid from sight as if their Devil God had swallowed them up and welcomed them into hell...

BETRAYAL IN THE CARDS

Adolfo did a tarot card reading on April 18th, 1989 and supposedly foresaw a betrayal among his followers. He knew that any of the many low level drug runners could have ratted out Serafin Sr and he now looked at his followers with a suspicious eye. He kept a gun close by and did his best to avoid sleep. His paranoia led to angry outbursts against his acolytes.

"They cannot kill you," he warned. "But I can."

The Commandante, Juan Ayala, meanwhile, took the threat of Constanzo's *brujeria* (witchcraft) very seriously.

"He flew in his own brujo (male witch), to take care of him and to take care of all his agents," Gavito said. "To make sure there was not 'bad vibes'. And not only that, but to help him in the investigation. To find out what was the best way to catch Constanzo. He (the witch) told Benitez, 'you wanna catch him? Burn their hut! Burn their nganga! Burn where they were worshiping.'"

"So we got out there one Sunday morning. Took one Mexican television station to cover it because he wanted Constanzo to see this. The brujo puts gasoline around it. They light it up and it starts to burn and we sit there while the whole thing burns to the ground."

Adolfo watched the scene on television as Ayala had hoped. His screen police sifted through what was left at the ranch. He then went into a rage inside the small hideaway apartment, smashing furniture and flipping over the couch for starters.

"He felt raped," Gavito said. "He felt that we had invaded his privacy. That we had done something we shouldn't have. He started losing it."

MOVING ON

Adolfo made one last move with his followers as they found an apartment on Rio Sena in Mexico City.

Sara, finally realizing her life was in danger or needing to now play the role of the victim since the authorities were no doubt closing in, made a handwritten note. She threw it out the bedroom window in the hopes that a Good Samaritan would come along and find it.

The note read:

Please call the judicial police and tell them that in this building are those that they are seeking. Tell them that a woman is being held hostage. I beg for this, because what I want most is to talk—or they're going to kill the girl.

A stranger walking by picked up the note but kept it to himself, thinking it was a joke. Upstairs, however, Adolfo plotted his next getaway move.

"They'll never take me," he said.

MORE RANDOM LUCK

A few days later, police arrived on Rio Sena and began going door to door looking for a missing child. Adolfo saw them from his window and began opening fire with his Uzi not realizing that they were not looking for him.

Over one hundred eighty-police men almost immediately. A fiery battle ensued which lasted almost forty-five minutes. Surprisingly, the only person injured during the crossfire was an officer who was struck by Adolfo's first barrage.

According to Sara, Adolfo ordered his own killing, telling El Duby to shoot him and his right hand man, Martin Quintana Rodriguez.

"He lost it," Gavito said. "He turned on the stove. Put the money on the stove. Started burning money. He started throwing coins out. Just lost it."

"He went crazy, crazy," said El Duby. "He grabbed a bundle of money and threw it and began shooting out the window. He said everything, everything was lost. No one's going to have this money."

"He wanted to die with Martin," Sara said.

Adolfo soon realized he was trapped. He handed his Uzi to El Duby.

"He told me to kill him and Martin," El Duby said. "I told I told him I couldn't do it, but he hit me in the face and threatened that everything would go bad for me in hell. Then he hugged Martin, and I just stood in front of them and shot them with a machine gun."

The police entered the apartment with guns raised but Adolfo and Martin were already dead, their bodies slumped together in a closet. The three remaining cult members, El Duby, Orea, and Sara were captured.

Over twenty rounds were found in autopsied body, possibly indicating that the Mexican police had continued to shoot him port-mortem.

THE TRIALS

El Duby's case was open and shut. He had confessed to the two murders and had no reasonable defense. Sara, however, was a tad different as she initially proclaimed to be a victim but knew too much of the cult's ins and outs to not be considered an accomplice.

After the shootout, fourteen cult members in total were indicted for murder. In August of 1990, El Duby was convicted of the killing of Adolfo and Martin, getting a 35-year prison term. Juan Fragosa and Jorge Montes were convicted to 35 years for the killing of Raul Esquivel.

Omar Orea, one of Adolfo's lovers, died of AIDS before going to trial.

Sara had been acquitted of Adolfo's slaying but was sentenced to a six year term for her criminal associations. She maintained her innocence throughout, stating that she never practiced the *palo malembe* but a "Christian Santeria."

Showing a calm demeanor during her interrogations, Sara expressed sorrow for the murders of Kilroy and the other victims.

American law officials saw Sara as having a split personality. They knew that in private, Sara would lose her "charming aspect" that she revealed when she knew the television cameras were on. She reverted into another self, talking with relish in describing the cult's rituals.

"I would say she has three personalities," a Mexico City attorney general said. "One personality comes out and faces the cameras and denies any involvement in the human slayings, another emerges when she talks to police and the third one comes out when she talks to herself."

American Customs agent Oran Neck spent several days in Mexico City assisting the local police. "Sara has kind of lost touch with reality," Neck said after he questioned her. "Her dual personality is coming up pretty strong right now. When you talk to her without the TV cameras there, she's pretty truthful."

"She gives a lot of data with great detail to investigators. It seems like when the cameras come on, she kind of reverts back to this nice, young, clean-cut kid from Texas Southmost College."

"When the cameras were there, she was real nice," Lt. George Gravito said. "When she was with us, she was the same ol' witch."

SARA'S SENTENCE

"If I had known it (the cult) was like this," Sara said. "I wouldn't have been in it."

Six years after her criminal association sentence was up, Sara was tried again and convicted of several of the murders at the cult's headquarters. She is now serving 30 years in prison.

During an interview with SFGate, Sara claimed that she was tortured by Mexican police after her capture. She said she was stripped, blindfolded, hung upside down, beaten, had her toenails pulled out and was burned inside her vagina in and out. She claims the burns were so severe that a doctor told her she'd never have children.

She also remembers the police shoving her hands into Adolfo's autopsied body at the morgue.

They yelled at her to pull out his heart.

"There is your devil," they mocked. "There is your prince. Kiss him. Kiss him."

The Mexican authorities have denied these claims.

"The witch deserves everything she got," Lt. George Gavito said.

Mark Kilroy's parents have said they have forgiven her but do not want her released. "You have to control a mass murderer," said Jim Kilroy. "What are you going to do? Let her loose and have her murder other people?"

Even after the convictions, some murders from the time period have remained unsolved. Between 1987 and 1989, there were 74 unsolved ritual murders in Mexico City. 14 of these involved children. Adolfo's cult is connected to 16 but there has been no evidence to connect them to the rest.

"We would like to say, yes, Constanzo did them all," prosecutor Guillermo Ibarra said. "And poof, all those cases are solved. And the fact is, we believe he was responsible for some of them, though we'll never prove it now. But he didn't commit all of those murders. Which means someone else did. Someone who is still out there."

SUSAN ATKINS & THE MANSON CULT

Susan Atkins was one of the more notorious female members of the "Manson Family" headed by Charles Manson. She was part of a gang of serial killers that terrorized Southern California in the summer of 1969. Known as "Sexy Sadie" because of her occupation as a topless dancer, Susan was involved in eight of the nine Manson killings including the gruesome Tate/Labianca Murders. She would be sentenced to death which was later commuted to life in prison. Susan would be denied parole over eighteen times in becoming the longest-incarcerated female inmate in the history of California.

CHILDHOOD OF A KILLER?

Susan was born May 7th, 1948 in San Gabriel, California. She was the middle child of three children born to Edward and Jeanette Atkins. Susan grew up in a middle-class area in San Jose, California. Her personality was described as "quiet" and she sang in both her school's glee club and the church choir. She appeared to have been the odd one out of the family, however. She had two other brothers and her parents would favor her brothers over her. Her father preferred the company of the eldest son while her mother preferred the youngest child, Steven.

"I didn't like my mother," Susan said. "She tried to get along with me, but I just refused to get along with her. I didn't like my father either. Didn't like either one of them. I didn't like my mother because she was an alcoholic. My father also was an alcoholic, used to beat my mother up."

"The family appeared to be middle-class," forensic psychologist Paula Orange said. "And the claim of the parents being alcoholics came from Susan herself. But it is evident that she had a normal upbringing for that era in that she was taken to Sunday school, sang in the church choir and was a member of the Girls Scouts. Not exactly a recipe for a future serial killer."

Her mother would die of cancer when Susan was fifteen. Susan and members of her church choir sang Christmas carols under her mother's bedroom window right before she would be hospitalized for the final time. Susan's relatives, however, remarked at how indifferent Susan was about her mother's death.

"As is the case with a lot of serial killers," Orange said. "There is a traumatic event in their lives that numbs them. They lose the ability to feel empathy for others. When Susan's mother died, it set the stage for her later life and made her vulnerable to the likes of Manson."

Susan was forced to move several times and wound up fending for herself at the age of eighteen. The cost of her mother's medical bills took a toll on her father financially and he was forced to sell their family home. Her father would move to Los Banos, California taking along Susan and her younger brother Steven. He would work on the San Luis

Dam construction project but would leave the two teens to look after themselves.

Susan would take a job during her junior year in high school, using the money to support herself and Steven. Academics were not her forte, however, as she was only an average student in Leigh High School in San Jose. When she entered Los Banos High School she had lost complete interest and received bad grades as she bounced from relative to relative.

"She (Susan) just didn't seem to care," stated a friend of Susan's. "Like when her mother died, she didn't show any real sadness about it. I don't think Susan cared about anything very much. There was something wrong with her"

Susan would leave home the moment she turned eighteen. She would work as a waitress in San Francisco and meet a pair of shady characters named Al Sund and Clint Talioferro. She joined the duo as they stole a Buick Riviera and then drove north up to Salem, Oregon. The trio would hide in the woods and steal food from other campers. A month later, the Oregon State police caught up with the Susan and her car thief friends. She was jailed for three months then placed on two years probation. Susan then returned to San Francisco, once again turning to waitress duties. Needing more money, she began doing some topless dancing as well as doing some housekeeping for rich people on Muir Beach.

While living in San Francisco, she stayed in a communal house and started taking LSD. She then dabbled in Satanism and other alternative lifestyles and philosophies.

She would then meet the man who would change her life forever, Charles Manson.

ENTER THE PSYCHO

Manson was playing guitar at a home where Susan lived with a few friends who were dope dealers. Janis Joplin lived near the house and Atkins enjoyed sitting on the front porch to listen to Joplin practice. Manson himself began singing songs to her when they first locked eyes.

"My eyes landed instantly on a little man sitting on the wide couch in front of the bay windows," Susan recalled. "Without moving his head, he opened his eyes and stared directly into my face. I stared back. It was thought our minds were speaking."

Susan then put on a Doors record and began to dance.

Manson came up behind her and placed his hands on her hips. The two strangers began dancing, with Manson leading his new friend with slow, sensual movements.

"He whispered in my left ear," Atkins would write in her memoir. "That's right. That's good. In reality, there's no repetition. No two moves, no two actions are the same. Everything is new. Let it be new."

Susan then described their dancing as a transcendental encounter. "This stranger and I were dancing, passing through one another. It was as though my body moved closer and closer to him and actually passed through him. I thought for a second that I would collapse. What had happened? Was I crazy? It was beyond human reality."

They made love and Manson told Susan to pretend that he was her father as they had sex. This made Susan even more attracted to him. "You are beautiful," Manson whispered. "You are perfect. You must break free from the past. You must live now. There is no past. The past is gone. There's no tomorrow."

Susan would then describe Manson in messianic terms, comparing the cult leader's treatment of his disciples to Jesus Christ. He washed her feet. He showed her affection and told her to love herself. Manson played the role of savior and father figure to the hilt.

"Charlie had instantly seemed more of a father to me than my own father," Susan said. "He played me like a yo-yo, first hugging me and praising me, then demeaning me in some way."

The house would be raided a few weeks after and Susan found herself homeless. Manson caught wind of her situation and invited her to join his "family". Susan then informed her probation officer that she would be going on a trip with a traveling preacher named Charlie. She and seven other girls, two of whom were pregnant got into Manson's black spray-painted converted school bus on a trip to Los Angeles. The probation officer nixed the idea but Susan ignored the request and was soon traveling down the coast with Charles Manson in the driver seat, singing made-up songs as he made his way down south with the wayward girls of the Haight-Ashbury district.

A NEW NAME

Manson christened Susan with the nickname of Sadie Mae Glutz and had someone create a fake ID for her. Susan then settled in the rest of the "Family" at the Spahn ranch, a former movie set where the followers would get free rent in return for the upkeep of the place.

"There was a semblance of unity," Susan said of her attraction to joining Manson's Family. "An ambiance of family camaraderie. Where everybody supposedly loved each other. There was a surface image of loving one another and caring for one another and being there for one another. And it appeared that way on the surface. And there was a lot going on underneath. You had a lot of different personalities. Lot of different personal problems, conflicting with one another but there was an image of commune."

Susan became one of the female leaders at the commune, often driving around other members. She bought into all of Manson's bizarre theories such as Helter Skelter, the creation of a revolution where the blacks would rise up and kill whites. The followers were subject to daily rantings and pronunciations from Manson as he would brainwash them into accepting his worldview.

"There was a lot of deprogramming that was involved in that," Susan said. "You take away a person's conscience of right and wrong by telling them while they're under LSD or any mind expanding drug, there's no such thing as guilt. And you've already come to a place in your mind or imagination where you don't like the feeling of guilt so its easy to say 'yeah, there's no such as guilt, I believe there's no such as guilt, therefore, I could do anything and not feel guilty about it.'"

PREGNANCY

Susan would bear a child by a man named Bruce White aka Bluestein. Manson would have the honor of naming the boy and he christened the baby as Zezozose Zadfrack Glutz. Manson was not happy with the pregnancy, however, up until the point, Susan was about to give birth.

"The baby is coming," Susan announced to the family with excitement.

"The baby isn't due for a few weeks," Manson snarled. "Go boil me some water. I gotta shave."

Susan then did as she was told and set up the shaving mirror for him in the bathroom. She then dropped to the ground and went into labor as Manson continued to shave.

The baby was breeched and one of the arms came out first. Manson then broke into song as did the other Family members, using the Beach Boys coda to "Cease to Exist/Resist."

It was after the birth of her son that Susan began to think about leaving the cult. Her rebellion began to be targeted toward Manson himself as she thought about her son.

"Things were getting crazy at Spahn's Ranch," Orange said. "Things were getting nuts. And I had a son. And I wanted to get away, I wanted to take my son away. I, on three separate occasions, went outside Spahn's ranch on my own in an attempt to get someone to come back and get my son."

Manson threw Susan out of the family and kept the baby with him and the Family.

"I had gone into Hollywood," Susan said. "Picked up some guy. I don't even remember the man's name. But he had a car, he had an apartment, I told him I would love him, take care of him, take care of his house if he would help me get my son. I went back to the house which was not at Spahn's ranch at that time, there was a house in Chatsworth. I told the young man if you'll wait out in the car I'm going to go in and I'm going to get my son. I didn't think Charlie was there. And I went into the house and there was different people there. Catherine Sher was there, Mary Brunner was there, Lynnette Fromme was there, Sandra Good was there, Tex Watson, Bruce Davis might have been there. Steven Grogan was there. And when I went in, I asked Catherine Sher, who at that time I called 'Gypsy', I said 'Where's my son?' and she said 'He's right here." And she reached over and someone else had him and I said 'Give him to me!' And I went to the closet where I knew there were diapers and blankets and I had my son and I was going to leave. And at that point Charles came down from the upstairs, it was a two story house and he asked me 'Where are you going?' I remember my heart really starting to pound and he said 'Before you go I want to show you something.' And he opened the bedroom door. And I saw Mary Brunner on a bed, she had two black eyes, her nose was swollen, she had a bloody lip, she was holding her sides and Charlie looked at her and said 'Tell her what you were gonna do this morning.' And she looked at me and said, 'I was gonna take Pooh Bear,' which is what she called her son, 'And leave.' And Charlie looked at me and said, 'Now do you want to go?'"

Susan would leave again, spending some time living at a communal home on the Buchanan Ranch in Topanga Canyon while hooking up with a man named Rory. Susan reportedly began talking bad about Manson to some of the people at the ranch. But one day Manson came to the ranch, standing above a ridge yelling 'Sadie!', his created name for Susan.

Susan then came running back to Manson as he welcomed her back into the Family. He then wrote a song called "Sexie Sadie".

"Sexy Sadie," Manson sang. "You came along to turn everybody on. Sexy Sadie, you broke the rules, you laid it down for all to see."

Susan was relieved of her parental rights after she was convicted of the killings. No one in her extended family sought custody of Zezozose and he was subsequently adopted. The child was renamed and Susan never saw him again.

"He was unscathed by all of this," Susan said. "And I'm so very, very grateful for that."

CRIMINAL WARM-UPS

By the summer of 1969, the Manson Family were pushing the envelope when it came to committing crimes.

They started with stealing cars. Susan learned the methods of auto theft rather quickly. She set the Family record for hot-wiring a car as she reportedly could do it in less than thirty seconds. But the Family were also suspected of possibly running a prostitution ring with all of the underage runaways that populated the Spahn Ranch. Manson had his followers sell drugs and during a deal gone bad Manson had an altercation with a black drug dealer named Bernard "Lotsapoppa" Crowe. Manson thought that he had killed Crowe and that the Black Panthers would seek to avenge his murder. He was wrong on both counts but he pressed the need for money on his followers. Manson then heard through the grapevine that one of his old friends, a man named Gary Hinman, had just come into a large inheritance. Manson sent his followers over to Hinman's home in order to entice him to join his cult and be its financial benefactor.

Gary Hinman was thirty-two years old at the time and made his living teaching music. He was on his way to earning a doctorate in sociology at UCLA. A practicing Buddhist, he owned several cars which included the obligatory hippie Volkswagen. He was a popular fixture in the Topanga Canyon area and was well known in the hippie subculture of Los Angeles.

Susan Atkins joined Bobby Beausoleil and Mary Brunner to Hinman's home on July 25th, 1969. Susan knew that their goal was to get money from Hinman and that the possibility of violence was all too real.

"There are competing stories from Susan about the Hinman murder," Orange said. "Initially, she told authorities that she did not know that Hinman was about to be killed. But in her memoir, she contradicts that claim. She comes clean after the fact because it would probably seem pretty silly for someone to arrive at a home with a bunch of knives and guns and not think that something bad was about to happen."

The three family members would confront Hinman about his rumored inheritance. Hinman would be puzzled by their sudden interest, denying that he had come into any riches. Beausoleil then beat Hinman to a pulp but the man would not change his tune.

Manson arrived at the home and wasted no time.

"I got a knife on my leg," Manson said. "And I cut Hinman's ear. I looked at them and I said 'That's how you do it. Don't bring me here, no more.' Then I'm thinking I gotta scare this character. I am what they call in the Underworld a bad actor. So I say, 'Alright, now I got to kill you, Hinman.' He said 'Don't kill me.' I said 'If I don't kill you, you are going to tell my parole officer and sent me back to prison."

Manson then threatened Hinman with more bodily harm if he went back on his word. Agitated and worried that he would be sent back to jail, Manson left Hinman's home with his Family members now in charge of the hostage.

"You guys stay here," Manson ordered Susan and Mary Brunner. "Fix him up a bit. Bandage up his ear."

Susan looked on horrified at the scene. Blood spewed from Hinman's ear as he rocked back and forth in pain, his entire face swollen from the beating. The two women put Scotch tape over Hinman's ear until they received more instructions.

The three Manson associates would keep watch over Hinman for two days until he signed over the registration for his cars. Manson then called Beausoleil on the phone and ordered him to kill Hinman.

Beausoleil would stab Hinman twice, fatally wounding him. He then left a bloody hand print on the wall as well as some Black Panther inspired revolutionary words. He did this in the hopes of pinning the crime on the radical group but he would instead be arrested eleven days later, caught sleeping in Hinman's car. After eleven days, Beausoleil was wearing the same bloodstained shirt that he wore while stabbing Hinman to death. Police would find the murder weapon hidden in the tire well of the car's trunk.

SHARON TATE MURDER

Manson would order Susan, Linda Kasabian, and Patricia Krenwinkel to accompany Tex Watson on the night of August 9th, 1969.

"Where are we going?" Susan asked as the three women piled into the car with Watson at the wheel.

"We're going to a home to get some money from some people," Watson said. "Then we're going to kill them. No matter what they do or say, do not show any mercy. No matter how much they beg, do not give them any leeway."

Steven Parent would be the first victim.

An eighteen-year-old delivery man, Parent was visiting the home on Cielo Drive as the previous month he had met William Garretson who was the caretaker at the mansion. Garretson invited Parent to visit anytime and the young man stopped by to try and sell Garretson an AM radio. Garretson refused but the two had a beer and Parent started to leave in his father's truck. As the gates opened for him to leave, he heard a voice yell "Halt!"

Tex Watson and the Manson Family were on him instantly. Parent put his hands up as Watson sliced down on him with his buck knife. The attack slashed off Parent's watch and cut through tendons on his hand.

"I won't tell!" Parent screamed in vain.

Watson then shot Parent four times and instructed the women to push his car back up the driveway. Watson walked across the lawn. The group then spread out and looked for any open window. Finding none, Watson cut through a screen window and entered the home. Once inside, he opened the front door and let in the three women.

Inside the home were Sharon Tate, Jay Sebring, Voytek Frykowski and Abigail Folger. Watson ordered the four people to lie face down on the floor. Sebring, a celebrity hair stylist, protested to Watson.

"She's eight months pregnant!"

Watson said nothing as he shot Sebring.

Incapacitated from the bullet wound, Sebring was kicked in the head several times by Watson. He would suffer a broken nose and eye socket. Watson would also stab him seven times.

"I remember when we first came in one of the people said 'who are you?'" Susan recalled. "And then Tex said 'I'm the devil and I'm here to do the devil's business. And I remember in my conscience it is so alive in me, I remember I had gone so far and there was no turning back. Even if I wanted to run, even if I wanted to leave, I couldn't. It was like I was caught in something that I had no control over. I had absolutely no say-so in what was happening there, I was like a tool in the hands of the devil is the only way I can put it

"I tied Voytek Frykowski's hands with a towel," Susan said. "And was instructed to kill him. And I raised the knife I had in my hand and couldn't put the knife down. I couldn't bring it down. It was like there was a force there that held my wrist. I couldn't-I couldn't move. And as he saw that I couldn't move then he very easily undid the ties that I tied his wrist with and he and I remember I was screaming for help and he was screaming for help and then Tex came and helped me and I just remember people scattering into different places." Frykowski tried to escape, running across the lawn. Susan and Tex Watson caught up with him as Watson finished him off with a flurry of stabbing. Susan stabbed at his legs. Frykowski tried desperately to stay on his feet, he grabbed a lamppost to try and remain upright. Susan and Tex were merciless, however. An autopsy would later reveal that he would suffer thirteen separate blunt-trauma wounds to his head, two gunshot wounds, and fifty-one stab wounds. Susan and Tex then returned to the home to finish with the killing of Sharon Tate.

Susan held Tate in a headlock while the rest of the occupants were being sliced and stabbed.

Saving her for last, Tex came upon the beautiful actress.

"Hold her down," Tex said as Susan grabbed Tate's legs.

"Please let me go," Tate pleaded. "All I want to do is have my baby."

"Woman," Susan said. "I have no mercy for you."

Susan would later write the word "PIG" on the front door using Tate's blood.

"We wanted to do a crime that would shock the world," Susan said. "That the world would have to stand up and take notice."

The Tate house had been chosen at random but Manson had known of the home from a year prior as it belonged to a record producer named Terry Melcher. Melcher had given Manson some false hope on a record deal that didn't come through.

The next night, Manson expressed his displeasure at how the murders of Tate and the others in the Beverly Hills home were sloppy.

"I need to show you people how it's done," Manson said. He summoned Susan, Patricia Krenwinkel, Tex Watson, Leslie Van Houten, Linda Kasabian, and Steve "Clem" Grogan to accompany him to their next target.

Manson and his followers would enter the home of Leno LaBianca and his wife Rosemary in Los Angeles. LaBiance was a hard working owner of a grocery store while his wife owned an antique shop. Breaking into their home while both were sleeping, Manson had Watson tie the couple up. Both husband and wife protested but Manson lied to the couple, saying that they were only there to rob them. Getting their compliance, Manson went back to the car and ordered Krenwinkel and Van Houten into the home.

"Do what Tex tells you to do," Manson said to the young women.

The Family would proceed to murder the couple and write revolutionary words on the walls using the blood of their victims.

TROUBLE AT SPAHN RANCH

On August 16th, 1969 the police would raid the Spahn Ranch on car theft charges. They still had not connected the Manson family to the Tate or LaBianca murders. The auto theft charges were eventually dropped and the members of the Family who had been arrested were released.

But Manson saw the noose tightening and decided to move his base of operations to Barker Ranch. Two months later, however, the police would raid the new location and arrest the Family once more.

It was during this time that a member of the family would rat out Susan for the Hinman murder.

Susan Atkins would be charged for that crime.

Now in prison, Susan would talk about her crimes to two of her fellow inmates, Virginia Graham, and Veronica Howard.

"I stabbed that bitch (Sharon Tate)," Susan said. "I said 'Look, bitch, I don't care if you're going to have a baby. You better be ready. You're going to die, and I don't feel anything about it. Then I tasted her blood."

Thinking she was crazy, the two inmates decided to report her confession to the authorities anyway.

Based on this information, the police would proceed to arrest Leslie Van Houten, Tex Watson, Linda Kasabian and Patricia Krenwinkel.

Susan would agree to be a witness for the prosecution if she could be spared the death penalty. But she would testify in front of the grand jury without this deal in place and informed that she might incriminate herself.

"I understand this," Susan said. "My life doesn't mean that much to me, I just want to see what is taken care of."

But before the case went to trial, Susan decided to severe ties with the prosecution. She would backtrack on her initial grand jury testimony in which she would admit to killing Frykowski and helping Tex Watson kill Sharon Tate. Susan would later say that she was influenced by Manson to not testify against him.

Contradictions remain in Susan Atkins' involvement in the Sharon Tate murder. Tex Watson would later state that he was responsible for all of Tate's wounds. He would dismiss Susan's confession as nothing more than an exaggeration to get attention. But another Family member, Barbara Hoyt, would eavesdrop on Susan on one occasion and overhear her cheerfully describe her role in the murders.

Susan would be part of the main Manson trial that commenced on June 15th, 1970. The media would locate Susan Atkins' father, Edward, and he dismissed the notion that Susan was under the influence of Charles Manson. Instead, he blamed drugs and the leniency of her previous sentencing. "I think she is just trying to talk her way out of it," Edward said. "She's sick and she needs help." Edward would reveal that he had tried for several years to get the courts to keep his daughter off the streets but they kept letting her go.

Susan would testify that she stabbed Sharon Tate as well as Tex Watson. She would claim that she did it because she was "sick of listening to her, pleading and begging, begging and pleading." Susan would continue to run interference for Manson, denying him any active role in the murders.

Susan's testimony was given little credence as she and the other "Manson Girls" would show their disdain for the proceedings. They would sing Manson inspired folk songs as they entered the courtroom and giggle throughout the trial.

Jurors were not impressed with her zany courtroom behavior. Susan would be sentenced to death and transported to the newly created women's death row in April of 1971.

HINMAN TRIAL

Susan was then convicted of the murder of Hinman, pleading guilty to all charges levied against her. She would testify that she didn't know that Hinman was about to be beaten up, robbed and possibly killed. Susan would later contradict this in later interviews and a memoir which is why so much of her testimony is given little credibility.

JAIL TIME

Sentenced to death, Susan caught a break in the legal system as the California Supreme Court struck down all death sentences in the state that occurred prior to 1972. Susan's sentence was then commuted down to life in prison.

In 1974, Susan would claim that she saw a vision of Jesus Christ in her jail cell. She converted to Christianity and became active in various prison programs. She began teaching classes and received letters of commendations after she helped out in two medical emergencies inside the prison (she helped intervene in a suicide attempt.) Susan would then publish a memoir and try to serve God with the same fervor that she served Manson. In her letters, she compared herself to the biblical Paul and Moses.

Susan would marry two times during her prison sentence. The first marriage would be with Donald Lee Laisure in 1981. Donald was known as "Flash" as he always carried around a huge wad of cash. He was also a congenital liar, lying about his military service in which he claimed a Navy Cross, Silver Star, and an Air Medal while "serving" 54 years. Susan would divorce him, stating that "he wasn't completely truthful with me." She would be his 35th wife. In 1987, Susan would marry James Whitehouse, a Harvard Law grad who would represent her at her parole hearings in 2000 and 2005.

The two would lobby hard in her final parole hearings to no avail.

"You know a person by their behavior," Susan said. "And my behavior in this institution speaks to the change that occurred over thirty years ago. I'm not the same person I was when I came in here."

Susan's parole hearings would continue to be greeted with deaf ears from the parole board. Sharon Tate's sister, Debra, would speak at Susan's parole hearings. She would read from a prepared statement from her father who described how their family was ripped apart. Tate's mother would spiral into a deep depression while her father, an Army colonel, would grieve in silence.

"There is no argument I can make," Susan said in response to Paul Tate's words. "I can only make every attempt to apologize. Remorse and sorrow for hideous actions is not calculatable. You can't calculate it."

Susan would then make references to her own repentance, using the standard rhetoric on how she should be judged for turning away from her behavior rather than be judged for her past actions.

COMPASSIONATE RELEASE?

Susan would fail once again at her 17th parole hearing in 2005. But by 2008, she had been diagnosed with brain cancer. The prognosis was grim, Susan already had one leg amputated and was given less than six months to live. This prompted a motion for Susan to be given a compassionate release which was denied on September 2nd, 2009.

Twenty-two days later, Susan would die at the Central California Women's facility in Chowchilla.

In her final moments, she had someone read Psalm 23 from the Bible to hear.

Her final words were "Amen.

SQUEAKY FROMME & THE MANSON CULT

Covering the tragedy of the Sharon Tate and LaBianca murders of the late 1960's, this book documents the twisted spiral of Lynette "Squeaky" Fromme. This book explores how the relatively normal world of Californian suburbia that Lynette Fromme was born into could lead her into the arms of the most notorious cult leader and cult group in history. Taking into consideration how the warped beliefs of a street hustler named Charles Manson could have such a pull on her and the rest of the Manson Family. Come along with us as we explore Fromme's role in the crime and times of Charles Manson and how this troubled young woman would eventually make an assassination attempt on the life of a United States President. She was an average American girl but something, somewhere along the way went terribly wrong. This book attempts to answer the question; what happened to Lynette Squeaky Fromme?

Introduction: What's the Problem?

The year was 1967. The war in Vietnam was just heating up, the Civil Rights movement was fully mobilized, and protesters were arriving en masse in opposition to the conventions of the day. But even with all of the political axes to grind, in 1967, the 18-year-old "Squeaky" Lynette Fromme was just a lost little girl wanting to find a way back home.

When the ex-convict and aspiring cult leader Charles Manson found her, she was weeping on a bench, depressed and frightened after her latest go round with her authoritarian father had left her homeless and on the street. Manson who—of all things—had taken coursework in prison that was based on the motivational book "How to Win Friends and Influence People" already knew how to win friends and he certainly could influence people.

Manson had finely honed his powers of manipulation and his ability to read others all the way back in his Juvenile Hall days in Indianapolis, Indiana. He developed a great capacity to infer what those around him wanted to hear and see, and then copiously worked to give them just that, as he constantly worked over his guards, attorney's and even court judges with his concerted efforts at charisma.

Seeking to be a heavily refined conman, it was a skill that seemed to serve Manson well, allowing him to charm his way through the parole board on several occasions. It was on his latest get out of jail free card excursion that he found Lynette Fromme drowning in her own tears on that public bench. And knowing exactly what to say, without any pretense or hesitation he instantly inserted himself in this troubled young girls world and cut through everything she was feeling so ill at ease about, by simply asking the question, "What's the problem?"

Chapter 1: The Family Business

The day Lynnette Fromme met Charles Manson she began a lasting partnership with the convict turned mystic. In truth, she became one of his first followers in what would become the "Manson Family". The group of free love drug addicted misfits who flocked to Charles Manson's promise of an alternative society. Manson often called himself the "Gardener" and fancied himself a caretaker for all of the misfit flower children of the 1960's who wandered his way.

The wacky beliefs that Manson expressed to his followers in the scorching hot heat of Death Valley were as laughable as they were stupidly offensive. Even worse than his wacky beliefs, however, was his inane ability to pull perfectly good rock music down into the derelict dumps with him.

Dropping acid and listening to Beatles records was one of Manson's favorite pastimes, and it was in the midst of this hobby of his that he somehow became convinced that the Beatles were prophets who had chosen to speak directly to him through coded messages in their music.

And the message that Manson fixated more than anything else, was the one he believed to have gleaned from a song called, "Helter Skelter" which Manson somehow believed to foreshadow future civil unrest and even ethnic cleansing. Shortly after the bloody murders in which Manson's brainwashed followers had scrawled the same two words on the walls with their victim's own blood, it would be Helter Skelter that would become the Manson Family's calling card.

Helter Skelter had become so associated with Manson and his crimes that it eventually forced former Beatles John Lennon and Paul McCartney to weigh in on the controversy. They really didn't know how Manson could have developed such a bizarre interpretation of their song.

Lennon contended that the title "Helter Skelter" was taken from an amusement park that had stood across the street from one of the venues they had played. The lyrics were really just a running gag reflecting the rides at the park with lyrics like, "When I get to the bottom I go back to the top of the slide, where I stop and I turn and I go for a ride."

Both John and Paul have always asserted that Helter Skelter never had much of a deep meaning at all, it was just the band getting together and playing a goofy, silly song. But for Charles Manson's disturbed mind it was some sort of twisted revelation. And as Charlie's loose associations with rock music and prophecy continued, his group of devoted followers, including one Lynnette Squeaky Fromme, became just as convinced as he was.

Convinced that the apocalypse was nigh, the Manson Family's original plan was to just wait it out in their own little commune in the middle of Death Valley, while society destroyed itself and then wait for the traumatized remnants of the civilized world to come crawling to them in the desert. Because who would the shattered remnants of civilization seek out to rebuild the world? Why Charles Manson of course.

It's all pure, unadulterated, tripped out insanity that makes as much sense as the paranoid schizophrenic who believed David Letterman was communicating to her through her television set. But for all of Charles Manson's insanity, he had a powerfully insidious charisma that had crept over his followers, and Squeaky Lynnette Fromme soon believed every warped word out of the madman's mouth.

And so it was that Lynette Fromme's new family spent the rest of the 1960's out in the desert waiting for the end of the world to arrive. But the end of their world didn't come in the form of societal collapse, the Manson Family's world would come crashing down around them when they were implicated in the murders of actress Sharon Tate and a couple name Labianca.

Even though his followers and Manson himself always contended that Manson had never actually killed anyone with his own hands, it was quickly believed that the twisted cult leader had inspired his followers to kill on his command. And in the aftermath of Manson's incarceration, it was Lynette Fromme who became his number one advocate, tirelessly showing up at court hearings, dictating his will and testament and incessantly speaking to reporters.

But much more than this, she quickly became the mouthpiece and the de facto leader of the Manson family in Charlie's absence. For the media at the time, it seemed that if Charles wasn't in charge, then well, Lynnette Squeaky Fromme most certainly was. The most well-spoken member besides Manson himself, Fromme quickly became a main focal point of media attention. According to Manson attorney Paul Fitzgerald, it was Lynnette who expressly formed the Manson Family's "heartbeat".

And for a time, even without Manson, Lynnette Fromme and many of her former Manson Family sister's tried to carry on, even recruiting more men who might serve as a surrogate for Manson. Lynnette attempting to emulate her hero preached to drifters and the discontented. But when men heard the words of Charles Manson's philosophies coming out of Lynette Fromme's mouth they often fell flat or seemed more like an offbeat form of amusement than any kind of real alternative in life.

Fromme would try her best to emulate Charles when she spoke of how the women's liberation movement had undercut American men disrupting the order, but when she spouted things like, "American women were wearing the pants, they had taken their men's balls and chained them up" something that would have had converts nodding along if they came from Charles Manson, just came off as absurd, offbeat, drunken humor when they came from petite little Lynette Fromme.

But while Fromme tried to secure her grip on the family, many in Charles Manson's legal team were attempting to secure their grip on Fromme. Manson's main defense attorney, "Paul Fitzgerald" insisted that Fromme was key to defending the case against Charles Manson.

And he began frequently meeting with Fromme, eventually designating her as a material witness in the case.

This was a move happily welcomed by Fromme since it meant that she would finally be able to visit the incarcerated Charles Manson. Fitzgerald meant to use these meetings as constructively as he could in order to bolster his defense, but much more than legal strategizing, for Lynnette Fromme these meetings usually turned into her own debriefing sessions for the family's former head.

Charles would prod her for information about the latest happenings with the family and then before she left, he would give her hundreds of commands and special assignments to carry out on the outside. If he wanted her to contact someone, she would, if he wanted her to discipline another family member she would, Fromme was now Manson's last window into the outside world and ultimately his messenger to the rest of the family and whoever else he wished to speak to.

But all of these seemingly obscure tasks, suggestions, and assignments that Fromme would receive from Manson none of them proved to have anything at all to the case at hand and attorney Paul Fitzgerald grew increasingly disconcerted. But as erratic as Fromme may have seemed, there was one area in which she always served to benefit the defense team and that was in bringing public awareness to the case.

From the beginning, Fitzgerald figured that the only way they could beat the system and win a not guilty verdict for Charles Manson would be to turn public opinion against the legal process itself. And in this task, Lynne Fromme was a ceaseless cheerleader. She once famously announced, "There is no love in that court, no God in the machine—just a lot of big words that swear to God and stagnate life, rather than adjusting justice, they make the court into a gladiator ring."

In her own jumbled and disjointed way, Fromme was making her own case to the public that the courtroom was like a modern arena in which men like her own modern day Spartacus; Charles Manson, were pitted against odds that were purposefully stacked against them. Fromme felt that if she could espouse this unfair treatment to the public she just might be able to shift the balance in Manson's favor.

So Fromme went on her own Charles Manson awareness campaign, and all over California she would proclaim to anyone who would listen, "Come to the trials—your trials—and see what's going on." This publicity campaign did manage to generate interest. And even if it was just out of morbid curiosity, people did come, so much so, that every courtroom seat was filled, and even outside the packed courtroom, curious onlookers crowded the scene.

But as the courtroom began to overflow with observers Fromme soon found herself without a seat of her own. The prosecution detesting the circus that had been created and viewing Fromme as a distraction would not allow her to attend. Since Fromme and her other acolytes were not allowed in the courtroom they decided to take their message to the street.

Practically every single day of the trial they would assemble on the corner down the street from the Justice Hall. Their antics became so much of a spectacle that they themselves became a morbid kind of tourist attraction. With people coming from miles around just to see Fromme and these other strange women who tried their best to keep up the family business.

Chapter 2: The Conviction of President's

For President Richard Millhouse Nixon, 1970 was proving to be an interesting year. The United States had just invaded Cambodia, greatly escalating a war Nixon had pledged to subdue, inflaming protests at college campuses all around the world. Just one month prior to this signing, 4 young protesters had been shot and killed by the National Guard at Kent State in Ohio. And then, of course, there was the ongoing trial of Charles Manson. A media circus that Richard Nixon freely commented upon on August 4th of 1970 when he declared in regard to Manson, "Here is a man who was guilt, directly or indirectly, of eight murders without reason."

Manson's guilty verdict made headlines across the national media the next day. One of the attorneys had brought a copy of of one of the newspapers to the courtroom proceedings that day, and Charles Manson seeing it, went berserk and snatched it up off the table, holding up for all to see Nixon's condemnation of him. Manson's efforts proved to be part out of outrage and out of cunning manipulation. Manson and his followers hoped that Richard Nixon's biased conviction could grant him a mistrial.

And sure enough, the next day, loyal Manson followers took the cue, and asked the judge, "Your Honor, the President said we are guilty, so why go on with the trial?" But trial judge Charles H. Holder was steadfast in his own conviction and suggested that Manson had brought the controversy on himself and then declared the attorney who brought the newspaper in the courtroom was in contempt of court for violating the order against newspaper publications being present during proceedings.

Lynnette Fromme who had already developed a cultivated hatred of the American Justice System was especially affected by Richard Nixon's pronouncement. She now felt it was clear that the system and even the very President of the United States were out to get them. This was a belief that she maintained and nurtured even after Nixon's replacement by Gerald Ford and many contend that this was what planted the seed of her desire to assassinate President Ford. She wanted to get revenge for the wrong she thought Richard Nixon had done them.

Manson himself tried to throw the President's conviction right back at him, when he declared in reference to Richard Nixon, "Here's a man who is accused of murdering hundred of thousands in Vietnam, who is accusing me of being guilty of eight murders." But no matter how Charles Manson tried to spin it, the proceedings would be destined to continue.

And now a new element of the case against Charles Manson began to merit the concern of the Manson followers; the prosecutions new star witness, former Manson Family member Barbara Hoyt. Barbara was a reluctant witness and had been pressured early on to testify. Wishing to hide from the whole affair she had contacted Lynne Fromme and other former family members, seeking advice as to where she could lay low.

Lynne and her cohorts then came up with the idea that she should fly to Hawaii with two other family members so she could avoid her court date. Apparently, Barbara initially agreed to the plan and flew to Hawaii with the two other members. It was here that Barbara began to have second thoughts, however, about whether or not she should truly avoid giving her testimony.

But before she could decide which way she was going to go with it, one of the member's gave her a hamburger drenched with enough LSD to send someone into a complete psychosis. Shortly afterward Barbara was found collapsed in the street mumbling about her courtroom duties to the lead prosecutor, stating, "Call Mr. Bugliosi and tell him I won't be able to testify today in the Sharon Tate trial."

Known as the "hamburger plot" Lynne and her others were quickly apprehended with charges of conspiracy and obstruction of justice. The lead prosecutor Vincent Bugliosi then did his best to convince the court that Lynn and her compatriots wanted nothing more than Barbara to either die or become permanently disabled from an overdose of LSD. Although the more serious charges were later dropped, Lynne Fromme and her cohorts were all hit up with a "conspiracy to dissuade a witness and conspiracy to bribe a witness" and thrown in jail.

It was from the depths of the Sybil Brand Correctional Institution for women that Lynnette Fromme was summoned once again to stand trial as a witness for the Manson defense team. During her testimony, she proved to be quite a burden for the Judge who had to snap her to attention and keep her on track with several yells of "Just answer the question, Miss Fromme".

From the outset, Fromme seemed more interested in using the witness stand as a platform from which to proclaim her views and the Manson family values than any recognizable form of usable testimony for the defense or the prosecution of a murder case. Growing increasingly frustrated, Judge Older soon silenced her words and ordered all counsel to a impromptu meeting with him in which he told Fromme's defense attorney, "this witness is not interested in being responsive to the questions asked her" and informed him in no uncertain terms that Fromme was not to, "use this court as a forum for her philosophies."

Whatever Lynn was trying to accomplish with all of her statements, it was to no avail, however, and all of the defendants charged with murder received an unequivocal pronouncement of death, while Lynne Fromme herself was quietly shuffled off to the Sybil Brand Institute for Women to serve the rest of her conspiracy charge. For most of America, the case against Charles Manson and his family was closed, but for Lynette Squeaky Fromme it was only beginning.

Chapter 3: Life outside the Pen

When Lynnette Fromme was released from the Sybil Brand Institute for Women in the year 1971, it seemed as if the whole world had changed; at least the world of Squeaky Fromme that is. Charles Manson was sitting on death row along with the other Manson Family members who were charged in the Tate and LaBianca murders. But for Fromme, it seemed that it was more than her friend's lives that had received a death sentence because it was her idealistic dreams—dreams that she had shaped with her fellow Manson family members—that seemed forever condemned to death as well.

The world she came back to was now unrecognizable, completely drained and empty of everything that she had previously hoped for. The summer of love which had flourished in Haight Ashbury with all of its promises was now lost forever. And the man who she looked to as a brilliant and wise father, the man they called the "Gardener" in the hopes that he could cultivate their minds for spiritual growth, was now forever ingrained in everyone else's mind as nothing more than a psychopathic killer.

When Fromme hit the streets after her release in 1971 she found a world gone cold that she no longer recognized. Most of her previous contacts had either disappeared or no longer wanted anything to do with her. For the rest of the year, Lynnette Fromme would bounce around from place to place and spend most of her energy writing a book about Manson which she hoped would somehow convince the world of his goodness and grant him a pardon.

Of course, none of this happened. Even when she finally finished her rambling monolog the story was so radioactive, even with the lure of media attention, no publisher was willing to touch it. Meanwhile, the legal system, or as Fromme and her colleagues frequently called it, "The System" seemed to be moving further and further away from them. As was made evident on October 21st, 1971 when Richard Nixon nominated the conservative Judge William Rehnquist to the Supreme Court.

But even so, Lynn still held out hope for a reversal of Manson's fate, one way or another and as a part of this, she started to establish her own contacts in the legal scene. One major part of this was her introduction in the Spring of 1972 to an up and coming San Francisco Attorney by the name of Doug Vaughn. A notorious figure in the region who drove a pickup truck and often sported a strangely Country Western look replete with hat and cowboy boots.

Lynnette maintained a rather superficial relationship with Vaughn and with him found sympathetic ears as she railed against the government she felt so betrayed by. Vaughn recalls one instance in which the topic came to the latest Democratic candidate for president, George McGovern, a conversation that led Fromme to make the blanket statement about politicians, "They're all just a bunch of liars and crooks."

But speaking of crooks it was soon Lynne Fromme who would develop a whole new cadre of crooks, liars, and thieves, who would ultimately implicate her in another notorious murder. Under the influence of Charles Manson who had forged a partnership with the prison gang, "The Aryan Brotherhood" a fresh flood of ex-cons came flooding into the Manson Family world.

During the course of these events, two of Lynne's friends were killed by the gang members and Lynne herself once again guilty by association was rounded up and thrown in jail once again as a result. It was here that her newly established legal consultant Doug Vaughn came to Lynette's rescue. After Vaughn investigated the case he discovered that the charges leveled against her had no weight.

From the police reports, he determined that the only reason the police brought her in was because she had hung out at the suspect's house and of course because of the tremendous reputation she had as the defacto leader of the Manson cult that already preceded her. The police had just hauled her in based on all of that. Lynn would finally have all charges once again dropped on January 2nd, 1973 and released back out on the streets of California.

Her freedom would not last long since the LAPD had a deep suspicion that Fromme had been involved in a robbery at a Seven-Eleven back in October of the previous year. And after being released from one prison system she was simply shipped off to another one, but in yet another amazingly ridiculous turn of fate in the annals of the Manson family, the "X" Lynn had first carved in her face years ago so that she would be spared from the wrath of locusts, managed to help spare Lynnette from serving another jail term.

Because after Vaughn had the witness to the Seven Eleven robbery take a look at the telltale mark, the witness finally conceded that the person she saw did not have such an unforgettable feature. A few days later the actual woman that robbed the store was captured and after she confessed to the crime Lynne was once again released to live life outside of the Pen.

Chapter 4: The Making of an Assassin

With her own legal battles finally settling down Lynette Fromme was struggling to find her place in the world once again. She was living off of $90 a month on welfare and found room and board at another cheap flat. Even though her surroundings were meager, and her outlook seemed bleak, many thought that she was finally trying to move on with her life and leave the Manson Family behind her.

But as fate would have it, a bestselling book would send her scrambling right back into the arms of extremism. Released in November 1974, Vincent Bugliosi published his book "Helter Skelter" which described the events that had become so infamous with the same working title. Fromme was still hurt over the fact that she could never get anyone to publish her own book, and then to find that someone else had beaten her to it was frustrating.

And then when she actually read the book for herself she was incensed to find certain passages that described her own presence and character in ways she found very upsetting. In one passage Bugliosi even seemed to call into question her mental capacity as he described Lynette Fromme and Sarah Good, "as if they hadn't aged but had been retarded at a certain stage in their childhood."

There it was for the whole world to see; Lynnette Fromme was mentally retarded, irrevocably stunted by Charles Manson who had snatched her up at 18 years old and warped her brain beyond recognition. This outrage spurned Lynnette Fromme to try once again to get her own book published so she could in her own words, "effectively combat the Bugliosi thought syndrome" and she now became utterly obsessed with telling her side of the story.

Meanwhile, President Nixon had resigned in disgrace and was replaced by Gerald R. Ford as the new President of the United States. Despite the seat change, however, it didn't take long for Lynette Fromme to redirect all of her anger at the "system" and Nixon, firmly on the linebacker shoulders of President Ford. She would tell a journalist at the time, "Ford is picking up Nixon's footsteps, and he is just as bad."

Donning her new cult uniform of a red robe Fromme then set out to shut down all of the ills that she claimed had been caused by government bureaucracy from Ford on down the line. One day she barged into a cement factory and demanded them to stop production because it was hurting the environment. In another instance, she even wrote a scathing letter to the Prime Minister of Japan criticizing him for Japanese Whaling.

At this point, calling herself a "Nun of the Earth", Fromme had given up men and embraced the environment, all the while claiming that she was ready to eliminate anyone that polluted the Earth. Even though many of her proclamations were startling with their degree of menace and violence, most people still did not take the petite form of Squeaky Lynette Fromme seriously.

In 1975 she heard that President Ford, the current embodiment of all her perceived evil was coming to town. It was an alignment of events that she just couldn't resist. Fromme remembers how disgusted she was with the excitement of everyone around her that the President was coming. Incensed with what she viewed as a gross and false form of adoration. At the time she intoned to her friend Sandra Good that President Ford was "a dummy, an empty head" and that his adoring fans were, "like sheep looking up to this dead head with dead thoughts."

With increasing rage and hatred that the whole city would turn out to see this "dead head" of a man, Lynette Squeaky Fromme determined that she would be the one to finally silence the object of her hatred once and for all. On September 5th, 1975 waiting with a crowd of, as she would put it, "adoring sheep" Lynette Fromme was the wolf in sheep's clothing, besides the brilliant red crimson of her dress she just looked like a small, pleasant-faced woman, waiting to see the President.

But when he came within just a few feet from Ford, as he was blithely shaking the hands of onlookers, President Ford saw Fromme move toward him out of the corner of his eyes. Ford assumed that she just wanted a presidential handshake as well, but when he stopped to look at the woman, instead of an extended hand to greet him, he saw a gun in his face instead.

After a momentary look of panic, President Ford scrambled to get out of the way of the deranged woman's line of sight, while Secret Service Agent Larry Buendorf screamed the ominous warning, "forty-five"!

Acknowledging the Colt Forty Five that the strange figure in red was waving in her hand Buendorf then pounced on Fromme and ripped the weapon from her hands as a seemingly puzzled and disappointed Fromme cried out, "It didn't go off!" For some reason the gun had failed to fire, granting a sad and dejected Lynette Squeaky Fromme yet another item to her growing list of failure.

Conclusion: Hiding From the Past

By the time of Lynette Fromme's attempted assassination of Gerald Ford, she had actually been quite used to getting arrested, being shuffled through the system and then ultimately being released. She had after all been found implicit with murder on two separate occasions already, and each time she was released.

And so it was that when her gone had failed to go off, preventing her from assassinating President Ford. Squeaky was subdued and believed that her charges would be dismissed since she "caused no harm."

But whether Fromme realized it or not, due to federal legislation enacted shortly after the assassination of President John F. Kennedy, assassination attempts came with a mandatory sentence of life in prison. But as much as she hated the system it would smile on her eventually, and she was released after just 34 years of her sentence in 2009.

Meanwhile, Charles Manson and the other family members are still in prison. Their death sentences were commuted when California abolished the death sentence, but they will no doubt be behind bars for the rest of their lives. But what about Lynnette Squeaky Fromme? Where is Lynnette Fromme now? The last anyone knew she was dodging the media, avoiding the limelight for a change, and trying to avoid anything and everything to do with her past.

LESLIE VAN HOUTEN & THE MANSON CULT

Leslie Van Houten is a former member of Charles Manson's "Family". She was convicted in 1971 for the killings of Leno and Rosemary LaBianca. Leslie's sentencing was part of the main Charles Manson trial but she blamed her actions on the control Manson had over her.

Houten, Manson and two other members of the "Family" were convicted and sentenced to death row until a new California law commuted their punishment to life imprisonment. Van Houten's lawyer passed away during the course of her trial and her convictions were thrown out. She then went to trial again, her primary defense being that she had a diminished mental capacity because of the drugs Manson had given her.

The jury remained deadlocked.

But Leslie would go to trial a third time. She would be convicted and sentenced to two life sentences.

Amazingly, after over twenty different hearings, the California state board decided to make Leslie eligible for parole.

On April 16th, 2016, Governor Jerry Brown agreed.

EARLY LIFE

Leslie was born on August 23rd, 1949 in Altadena, a suburb of Los Angeles. Her father, Paul, worked as a car sales auctioneer while her mother Jane was a former teacher turned housewife. Leslie grew up in a church-going family with one older brother and two adopted siblings who were Korean. A boy and a girl, they were orphaned in Korea and came to live with the Van Houten's in the southern California suburban home which had a pool.

"It was a middle-class experience if there ever was one," forensic psychologist Paula Orange said. "Leslie's family did all the right things. A two-parent household where the father worked and the mother stayed home and took care of the children. They had a home with a pool and would go to church on Sunday. Not exactly the type of background you would expect for a killer. Leslie did not come from an abusive home and seemingly had all she needed to become a happy, well-adjusted young woman."

Trouble started for Leslie at the age of fourteen when her parents divorced. Her mother was forced to go back to school to renew her teaching credentials. Her father left the home but he was no deadbeat dad. He stayed in touch and provided for all of the children financially. Leslie seemed to be well-adjusted on the surface, she was elected homecoming princess two years in a row. But she began dating an older man and by the age of sixteen, she had experimented with LSD for the first time. She would have an abortion as well as begin the drug habit, both of which would cause considerable emotional pain to herself and her family.

"I seemed to what more living out of life then what was expected of young girls at that time," Leslie said. "Drugs, sex, breaking away from the norm."

Leslie met another young man and the two ran away to the Haight-Ashbury district of San Francisco. She eventually returned to Southern California living with her father to complete her high school education. She enrolled in secretarial school, learning shorthand but the career didn't seem to be the right choice for her. Leslie began to study yoga and saw an alternative to her middle-class destiny when she broke up with her boyfriend and began living in a hippie commune in Northern California.

HIPPIES MAN

Leslie would meet Catherine "Gypsy" Share and Bobby Beausoleil, moving in with them in 1968. She would begin a dating relationship with Beausoleil who was a mainstay at the communes along the coast. Nicknamed "Cupid", Beausoleil was a reform school drop-out who managed to get some bit parts in low budget movies. He was also a promising musician, performing in two bands called "The Milky Way" and "Love."

Catherine "Gypsy" Share, on the other hand, was the stereotypical free spirit of the counter-culture movement at the time. Like Beausoleil, she dabbled in acting and got a bit part in a soft core porn called "The Ramrodder." Gypsy would talk of making a pilgrimage to hang out with a man who knew all about love and peace. A man who lived in the moment.

His name was Charles Manson.

"I had gotten to the ranch with people who were traveling up and down the coast," Leslie said. "And prior to that I was neck deep in the hippie movement and I met these people that said they came from a commune in LA where they lived for the day and for the moment and it was a lot of the Leary kind of philosophy of 'be here now'. I was attracted to that."

Leslie followed both Beausoleil and Gypsy to Manson's commune. She was part of the expansion of the "Family" which now included Tom "TJ" Walleman, John "Zero" Haught, Cathy "Capistrano" Gillies and "Simi Valley" Sherri. Gypsy and Leslie had cut ties with Bobby Beausoleil but Manson considered Bobby to be a friend. He didn't want to insult him by taking his women. After much convincing by Gypsy, Manson relented.

Initially, Manson did not want to accept Leslie into the fold. She had an intelligent air about her and he considered that to be a threat. He didn't need smart people. He wanted people who would obey.

Manson eventually saw the positive benefit in having Leslie join the "Family". She was beautiful and he had physical relations with her as part of her initiation. Her beauty would serve in helping recruit more male members. He saw that Leslie also had secretarial skills. He employed her to write in shorthand in order to record the lyrics of the songs that Manson would sing.

"I heard he (Manson) was like Christ," Leslie said. "That he had the answers and that I just really needed to go and meet him. As twisted as it all got I felt that I had met someone that by being around him would have a positive change."

"Leslie stayed for one night at the ranch," Orange said. "Then she returned a little under a month later to stay permanently. Manson, of course, took her under his wing with a lot of his quasi-Buddhist teachings like the shedding of the ego, the giving up of a personal identity. Leslie was at an age where she was vulnerable to that kind of mumbo jumbo. Manson would step in front of her and encourage Leslie to mirror his body movements, to try and anticipate what he would do next. He used these kinds of methods and more to get into his follower's heads."

Leslie called her mother telling her that she was "dropping out of society" and would not be in contact again. She then fully embraced all of Manson's hippie ideals; freeloading, eating out of garbage cans and drop acid.

"Leslie would later claim that she become such an acid head that she could no longer discern reality," Orange said. "She becomes exactly what Manson wanted. Someone who followed without question."

LIFE AT THE SPAHN RANCH

Manson's headquarters were based at the Spahn Ranch. The Ranch had originally been used as a movie set for many Western films. George Spahn was the owner of the ranch at the time. He was eighty years old and allowed the Manson Family to live rent free in return for doing chores and maintaining the ranch. The number of members continued to swell as the hippie movement grew.

"There were about fifteen or so solid members," Leslie said. "There were ten or so transients."

There were also considerably more women than men.

"Manson worked women better," Leslie explained. "I wasn't one of the ones that was physically enamored with him. I was more caught and mesmerized by his mind and the things he professed."

Manson charmed his acolytes with the idealistic philosophy of acceptance and free life. The ranch was isolated and Manson would be the only voice that members of the "Family" listened to. Barbara Hoyt, a fellow follower, would later describe Leslie as a "leader" at the Ranch while Manson was "The Gardener."

"I tend to all the flower children," Manson said.

Leslie became comfortable living at the ranch as she felt a lack of judgment and a kinship with the other followers. There were no clock watches, no sense of time and no sense of personal identities like individual names or birthdays.

"You could absolutely not talk about your past at all," Leslie said. "We started off, in the gentler days, to shed ourselves of our egos and to get rid of our own identity. We were to do what was then called 'become one with one another.' He (Manson) would do this by assaulting our families. Mocking our morals and all of the things we had been taught because all of us were middle-class Anglos."

"Manson's followers were all people who were raised in the church," Orange said. "So it is no coincidence he fostered a 'Jesus-like' look and manner in that he talked in riddles that seemed to make sense to them. He told his followers to love themselves and like Jesus, he would treat them with kindness, even going so far as wash their feet. He would rename his followers like a messiah renaming his family. Leslie would be called Lulu, Lou, or Morning Flower."

ENTER TEX WATSON

Tex Watson was an all-state high-school athlete who was a student at North Texas University. But while working as a baggage handler he began to become interested in the hippie movement and psychedelic lifestyle. His curiosity would eventually lead him to the commune of Charles Manson.

Like Leslie, Tex Watson saw Manson as a God-like figure. Manson would often ask his followers if they were ready to die for him. Watson, like the female followers, had been raised in church. He would later tell his mother that he found God when he met Charles Manson.

"You've always wanted me to be religious," Watson told his mother. "Well, I've met that Jesus you preach about all the time. I've met him and he's here right now with me in the desert."

When Manson asked Watson to kill for him, the former scholar-athlete would not hesitate.

"I didn't even have to think about it," Watson recalled. "(Manson was) like some mystic, so filled with the love of God that nothing is too great to ask, I was filled with Charlie. He WAS God to me."

"Sometimes he (Manson) would re-enact the crucifixion when we were on LSD," Leslie said. "And it was very realistic. He'd go through the whole thing (being nailed to the cross). Then he would make the connection between man's son and son of man. And then the questions would begin 'would you die for me?'"

The brainwashing continued on a daily basis. Manson, while not trained in mind-control techniques knew exactly what buttons to push to get what he wanted.

"One night at the ranch," Leslie said. "We're all sitting around in our little evening get-together. He started to say 'baa, like sheep' and every single one of us, did exactly at the moment that he said."

THE COMING RACE WAR

Manson began talking of a race war. He wanted to stage acts of violence that would propel the black community to follow him into "war" and extinguish the white race. He would have his followers train as if they were about to go into combat. There were guns on the ranch as well as numerous knife stabbing training sessions.

"I believed that Manson was Jesus Christ," Leslie said. "And that it (a race war) was something that had to be done. It was not something that I felt good about or that it was like war. We were going through combat training at the ranch. Prepped like that. He (Manson) believed that the whites had been on top for too long. And all they did was put harm on other people. That we were not like them and that the last time he came he had been crucified and this time he would have to make himself known."

Despite all of the terrorist-like talk, the followers would sit around the ranch all day naked and drop LSD. Manson, a former pimp, kept a lot of his male followers in line with the promise of "free love" from the female followers.

"If a man wanted you," Leslie said. "You went with him. You couldn't resist."

"I looked them in the eye and saw what they wanted," Manson said. "I told them what they had to do to stay with me. If they didn't like it, they left. If they stayed, I had sex with them. I told them to forget their hang-ups and guilt trips. They had to become one with me and my truth. Their wills had to die to become one with me. Sex was their initiation. It was a celebration of life's pleasures. Something to enjoy, not to be afraid of."

MUTINY IN THE FAMILY

Not all the followers rubber stamped Manson's every word. Pat Krenwinkel ditched the communed and hooked up with a biker. Manson tracked her down and ordered Krenwinkel to come back with him. Pat was shocked that she had been found and thought Manson used "special powers to find her." Truth was, Manson had several contacts in the biker culture that he employed.

Leslie herself began to question some of Manson's intentions. Angered, Manson pulled her aside and took her for a ride in his dune buggy. He parked at the top of the Santa Susanas and told her, "If you want to leave me, jump."

Leslie stayed.

There were a few defections in the commune but the primary people Manson needed, like Tex Watson and his "Manson Girls", all stayed.

ROCK STAR WANNABE

Another motive behind Manson's actions were his own failed pipe dreams. He was obsessed with becoming a rock star. He auditioned numerous times and failed miserably. Manson had his hopes for a record deal up when Beach Boy Dennis Wilson introduced him to record producer Terry Melcher. Wilson went so far as to record two of Manson's songs and Melcher expressed cursory interested in producing an album with Manson. He also wanted to make a film about the family and their communal lifestyle. Manson would audition for Melcher but the producer was unimpressed. They remain on cordial terms until Melcher saw Manson get in a fight at the Spahn Ranch with one of his followers. Melcher immediately parted ways with Manson, ceasing all communication.

This enraged Manson and according to Leslie, he "became angry all of the time."

"He felt rejected by the music industry that he wanted so much to be a part of," Orange said. "He adopted a few of the songs from the Beatle's White Album. Songs like Helter Skelter, Piggy, and Revolution 9 became his own personal anthems."

Piggy, in particular, became one of his favorites. The song spoke of white suburbia with their forks and knives.

"He thought one of the songs is supposed to say his name or something," Leslie said. "And we'd listen to it over and over and over. Number nine. Number nine. And you know he was really involved in Revelations 9."

One of his bizarre beliefs was that he believed that the Beatles would join the "Family" and "escape to a bottomless pit where they would becoming the proper rulers of the earth." Manson told his followers that the apocalypse from the Bible was forthcoming. He called the upcoming race conflict "Helter Skelter" from the Beatles' song.

"It was going to be a racially motivated revolution," Leslie said. "And that the blacks were going to control and take over the power."

With a record deal not in the cards, Manson began having his followers commit crimes. They started small at first by stealing cars and robbing homes. Leslie herself had robbed her father's home twice but was caught and served minimal jail time.

Manson would later shoot a member of the Black Panther party named Bernard "Lotsapapa" Crowe. Manson thought he had killed Crowe and began fearing retribution from the Panthers. This led to him training his "Family" members on how to kill with knives.

No longer confident in his ability to acquire fame through music. Manson sought a different route to becoming recognized.

He would become famous by killing people.

And Leslie went along for the ride.

THE FIRST MURDER

Manson's "Family" first targeted Gary Hinman, a music teacher. Details are sketchy on the motives of killing Hinman. Bobby Beausoleil would claim that the Family went to his home because he had cheated them on a drug deal. Another possible motive was that Manson believed that Hinman had money and cars. He wanted him to join the commune and thereby turn over his assets to his growing cult. Hinman refused and Manson sliced off his ear with a sword. Beausoleil stitched the ear back on with dental floss. Hinman was a pacifist and continually asked Manson "why are you doing this?"

After three days of torture, Beausoleil fatally stabbed Hinman two times in the chest. Manson's followers then wrote the words "Political piggy" on the wall with Hinman's blood. A little over a week later, Beausoleil would be arrested driving Hinman's car.

SHARON TATE MURDERS

In August of 1969, two members of the "Family" would be behind bars. Beausoleil and also Mary Brunner who was arrested for credit card fraud. Manson then targeted the residence of record producer Terry Melcher.

Only Melcher no longer lived there.

"Manson knew that Melcher no longer lived at the home," Orange said. "But in some strange, twisted way he probably thought he would be sending a message to the producer who doused his hopes of being a rock star."

The home was now owned by famed film director Roman Polanski who was out of the country at the time. Staying in the home was actress Sharon Tate, Votek Fryskowski, Jay Sebring and coffee heiress Abigail Folger.

Manson followers Tex Watson arrived at the home with three of the Manson Girls: Susan Atkins, Patricia Krenwinkel, and Linda Kasabian. Watson would lead the way while Kasabian stood watch outside.

Breaking through a window, Watson would go on a rampage inside the home. Within minutes would kill Frykowski, Sebring, and Tate who was eight months pregnant. Folger tried to escape but Krenwinkel caught her and stabbed her to death.

The killers stole a total of seventy dollars.

When they returned back to the ranch Manson confronted them at the front. He asked them "if they had any remorse." They said no and Manson reiterated that he and his followers were in a war and that they should not have any remorse for their actions against the enemy.

"Don't tell anyone," were his final words to his minions of death.

LABIANCA MURDERS

The next day, Manson again handpicked some of his followers to commit more murders.

"He (Manson) asked me," Leslie said. "Do you believe in me enough to know that this is something that has to be done?' Or something to that effect and I said 'yes, I do.' I didn't walk right up and say 'May I go?' But I think everything on my face said that."

Leslie went along with the murderous group that night.

She would join Manson, Tex Watson, Patricia Krenwinkel, Susan Atkins, Linda Kasabian and Steve "Clem" Grogan as they staked out a house in the city of Los Feliz.

The home belonged to Rosemary and Leno LaBianca. They had the misfortune of being neighbors with a Manson friend named Phil Kaufman. Kaufman had been another music executive who had interactions with Manson and did not help him advance his career.

"The thinking was," Orange said. "And this is supported by Susan Atkins' testimony, was that Manson wanted to put the fear of God into Phil Kaufman and every other music executive that rejected him. The LaBianca's happen to live in the wrong place at the wrong time."

Leno LaBianca was a well-to-do owner of a chain of grocery stores while his wife, Rosemary, owned a boutique. Rosemary had been deeply disturbed by the Sharon Tate murders and went to the bedroom to go to sleep. LaBianca stayed awake, laying on his couch but falling asleep as he read the sports page.

Manson entered the home first, calmly assuring LaBianca that they were only there to rob the place. He asked where the money was kept and if there were anyone else in the house.

Leno complied, telling them that his wife was in the bedroom and giving them what little money he had on hand. Manson produced a leather strap and tied up Leno's hands.

Leslie and Patricia Krenwinkel came upon Rosemary in the bedroom while her husband was being assaulted.

"Stop stabbing me!" Leno cried out.

Rosemary awakened, startled to see the two women in her bedroom.

"The minute I walked in the house," Leslie said. "It became clear that this was not what I had imagined. You know, before that it had always been an abstract kind of thing and when it was the real thing, I was absolutely torn in half."

Tex Watson placed a pillowcase around Leno's head then secured it with electrical cords from lamps in the home. He then began stabbing the man to death.

Leslie and Pat would hear the screams of Leno as he was being stabbed to death. They tried to hold Rosemary down as she called out for her husband.

"For a brief moment," Leslie recalled. "I realized that these are people that love each other."

Rosemary struggled to break loose as she heard the screams of her husband who was being stabbed by Watson.

"I tried to hold down Mrs. LaBianca as Pat stabbed her," Leslie said. "And I was confused and torn inside. I wanted to do what Manson had asked us to do. And I was battling in my own sense, I was battling something I was not capable of handling. And I didn't hold her down well. And she (Rosemary LaBianca) picked the lamp up and I don't even know if she even knew she had the lamp. She was struggling for her life."

Rosemary broke free, grabbed the lamp at swung it at Leslie.

Leslie fought with the woman and knocked the lamp away. She then held Rosemary down while Krenwinkel stabbed her in the chest.

The knife bent on Rosemary's clavicle and Leslie called for help.

"I don't remember if Pat said to me 'go get Tex' or if I just did," Leslie said. "I ran to Tex and told him that we were not capable or we were not able to kill her. At that point, Tex ran into the bedroom. I stood in the hallway and I looked into a blank room that was like a den."

Watson arrived and began stabbing Rosemary. He then handed Leslie the knife and ordered her to "do something."

"And I took one of the knives," Leslie said. "And Patricia had one knife, and we started stabbing and cutting up the lady."

"I promise I won't call the police," Rosemary said, her life ebbing away. "I won't call the police."

But her use of the word 'police' only egged Leslie on.

"And it seemed like the more she said 'police,'" Leslie said. "The more panicked I got."

Leslie then plunged the knife into the woman's back and buttocks anywhere between fourteen to sixteen times (LaBianca's body would later reveal that she had been stabbed over forty-seven times).

Watson then went into the LaBianca bathroom and took a shower. He then raided the refrigerator, getting cheese and chocolate milk for Leslie and Pat.

Krenwinkel then took a fork and stabbed the corpse of Leno Labianca repeatedly before writing different slogans around the walls in his blood. Words like "Helter Skelter," "Rise," and "Death to Pigs."

All because Manson wanted them to do something "witchy" after the job was down.

The word "War" was carved into Leno LaBianca's stomach.

Tex Watson then ordered Leslie to clean the house for fingerprints.

"I was very uncomfortable and I wanted out of the house," Leslie said. "Manson had told him (Tex) that everyone was going to change their clothes. I didn't have a change of clothes with me and I didn't have anything on my clothes. I asked Tex could I not change my clothes because I didn't need to and he said no, that Manson had wanted everyone to and for me to get clothes out of Mrs. LaBianca's closet and so I went and I found her clothes and I wore them."

Tex stole Leno's wallet which had a credit card inside. Manson ordered him to "leave it where a black person could find it" and then take the blame.

Leslie then hid in the bushes wearing Rosemary's clothes until morning. When sunrise came, all three hitchhiked back to the ranch.

THE AFTERMATH

Leslie did not watch the news broadcasts the next day.

"I went back to the back farmhouse," Leslie said. "It was a movie set and the back farmhouse was where many of us were staying. I went back to the back farm house and I burned the clothes. Tex had taken some money from the house and I was counting the money with Diane Lake. I don't know why he took it (the money) it wasn't a robbery."

Manson then sent Leslie and Krenwinkle to a place called "Fountain of the World." He was adamant on keeping the young women removed from the others at the commune as he didn't want them talking about the murders.

A motorcycle gang then snitched on the Manson followers and Leslie would be arrested in December of 1969. She was much more forthcoming on the crimes of the Family then the other followers, informing the police on who were the perpetrators of the Tate and LaBianca murders. She still tried to play cute during interrogations but ultimately ended up incriminating herself.

"What did you hear about the Tate murders up there?" the detective asked.

"I'm deaf," Linda said, laughing. "I didn't hear nothing."

"Five people were killed up there, on the hill. And I know three for sure that went up there. I think I know the fourth. And I don't know the fifth. But I suspect you do. Why are you holding back? You know what happened."

"I have a pretty good idea."

"I want to know who was involved. How it went down. The little details."

"I told Mr. Patchett. I'll tell him if I changed my mind. I haven't changed my mind yet."

"You're going to have to talk about it someday."

"Not today," Linda said. "How did you ever trace it back to Spahn?"

"Who did you see leave the night of the eight of August?"

"Oh, I went to bed early that night," Linda laughed again. "Really, I don't want to talk about it."

"Who went?"

"That's what I don't want to talk about."

"Tell me about the family," the detective said.

"You couldn't meet a nicer group of people," Leslie said. "I liked Clem the best. He's fun to be with. Sadie was really nice but she tends to be on the rough side. Bruce doesn't do anything but talk. I mean he won't do anything. He is always talking about blowing someone up but he won't do it. The Family is great."

"The family is no more Leslie. Charlie is in jail. Clem is in Jail. Zero killed himself."

"Zero!" Linda said in shock. "What happened?"

"They were playing Russian Roulette. Blew his brains out. Bruce Davis was with him.

"Was Bruce playing it too?"

"No."

"Zero was playing Russian roulette all by himself," Linda said, her voice dripping with sarcasm.

"Kind of odd, isn't it?"

"Yeah, it's odd."

"I know five people had gone to the Tate residence. There were three girls and two men. One of the men was Charles Manson."

"I don't think Charles was in on any of them," Leslie said defensively. "Only four people went to Tate.

TRIALS AND TRIBULATIONS

Tex Watson would not be tried at the main Charles Manson trial. Manson had been accused of being the mastermind of the murders but the only followers on trial along with him for causing were Leslie and Pat Krenwinkel.

During the trial, Leslie appeared to have been on an acid trip. She laughed inappropriately during testimony about the murders. She would take the stand and confess to committing the murders but denied that Manson had taken part.

Manson then carved an X on his forehead and Leslie copied him, which bespoke to the control he had over her. Leslie would fire three defense lawyers in a row as they wanted to blame her actions on Manson's control over her. Her defense lawyer had called an expert witness to the stand to talk about the effects of LSD on personal judgment, Leslie became livid.

"This is all such a big lie," Leslie screamed. "I was influenced by the war in Vietnam and TV."

On March 29th, 1971, Leslie was convicted of murder. She continued to try and defend Manson, testifying that he was not involved in the killing.

During her psychiatric evaluations, Leslie revealed that she had routinely beat her Korean adopted sister. Her psychiatrist called her a "psychologically loaded gun" and he did not believe the fact that Manson had control over her behavior nor had he brainwashed her as so many people believed.

Leslie showed no remorse for what she did to Rosemary LaBianca.

"Sorry is only a five letter word," Leslie said. "You can't undo something that is done."

Leslie would also concede that she could have stabbed Rosemary in the neck which would suggest that she inflicted wounds while the victim was still alive (Leslie remained vague in her testimony on whether or not Rosemary was still alive as she attacked her.)

SENTENCING

Leslie was then sentenced to death and would become the youngest woman ever executed in California. A special unit was built for her as no death row for women prisoners was in existence. But her death sentence was commuted after the California Supreme Court struck it down.

She would then eligible for parole after she had served seven years.

Prosecutor Vincent Bugliosi predicted that all three women followers would be released within fifteen to twenty years.

"All of the Manson followers, in particular, the women, thought they would get off light," Orange said. "Leslie herself thought that she would be out within seven years."

During her trial, Leslie reconnected with her family. She described them as angry and resentful but were reaching out nonetheless.

"I remember telling my mother that she would probably be better off just leaving me alone," Leslie said. "Because I had so easily left her life. She just said that she wasn't made of that kind of stuff."

Despite Leslie's initial attempts to cover for Manson, he did not have the same loyalty to her.

"I didn't know Leslie very well," Manson said. "She was a daddy's girl."

"Part of my job at the ranch was to read to him (Manson) from the Bible. And it's been a very difficult thing for me to find forgiveness. Spiritually. I guess I felt that I had gotten into this mess on my own and AA (Alcoholics Anonymous) talks a lot about God as we understand him and turning our will over to Him, removing defects of character. The more I studied the more I realized I needed to find some kind of peace with what had happened. Not just with the crime but life at the ranch and Manson in general and what he had done and the effect he had over me."

Seven years after the crime, Leslie was interviewed by Barbara Walters on national television.

"Is it something that you think of (as having) happened to somebody else?" Walters asked.

"No, it's very real to me," Leslie said. "It's very real to me at night when I'm alone in my cell with my thoughts. It's at that point that I-I don't try to block it out. That's part of the hell that I'll have to live with forever."

RETRIAL

Leslie was given a retrial in 1977. Her new defense had argued that she should have been given a mistrial when her first lawyer died (some believed that he was murdered by the Manson family.) Leslie's new attorneys argued vigorously for the fact that her mental faculties had been compromised due to her LSD use and Manson's psychological control over her. At trial's end, the jury remained deadlocked as they could not decide on whether Leslie's actions constituted a first-degree murder or a manslaughter.

PAROLE REQUESTS

The male followers of Manson have had moderate success at their parole hearings. Clem Grogan who helped Manson with the torture killing of Donald Shea, was paroled in 1985. An accomplice named Bruce Davis was given a parole board recommendation for release in 2010 but Governor Jerry Brown overruled the decision.

Leslie would be rejected by the parole board thirteen times. She would try seven more times and fail. During these hearings, she had disowned any ties to Manson and had articulated her remorse for the murders.

"Mr. and Mrs. La Bianca died the worst possible deaths a human being can," Leslie said at her last parole hearing. "It affected their families. It affected the community of Los Angeles, which lived in fear. And it destroyed the peace movement going on at the time, and tainted everything from 1969 on."

During her time in jail, Leslie wrote numerous short stories, edited the prison newspaper as well as doing secretarial duties.

"I feel that sometimes when I talk about it (the murders)," Leslie said. "I sound distant and removed. I don't make light of my crimes. I accept responsibility for what I did. I have spent years learning to live with it. As I sobered and grew away from Manson, living with my conscience with what I have done as been a very difficult thing for me...I understand the horrendousness of what I did. It is something that I live with every day."

"She knew what she was doing," Manson said in response. "She was a papa's girl and wanted to do her own thing. Now she blames me for helping her be herself."

On April 14th, 2016, Governor Jerry Brown approved Leslie's eligibility for parole.

PATRICIA KRENWINKEL

"It is countless how many lives were shattered by the path of destruction that I was a part of, and it all comes from such a simple thing as just wanting to be loved."

This is a statement made by Patricia Krenwinkel in her first interview in over 20 years. Her path of destruction that consumed not just her, but all the people she touched, arguably began in 1967 when her life crossed paths with Charles Manson.

Born in 1947 to an insurance-salesman father and a homemaker mother, Krenwinkel grew up in Los Angeles, California. Bullied at school and feeling rejected at home, she developed low self-esteem and often felt isolated and unloved. Her teen years happened to coincide with the 1960s. It was a strange time, with new movements and social upheaval that captivated American and left no home untouched. The Krenwinkel household was no exception. As the relationship between her parents began to deteriorate, her relationship with them did as well. During this time she became increasingly attached to her older half-sister who, while struggling to find her own identity, indulged in underage drinking and drug use. Searching for a place to belong Krenwinkel moved away to attend Spring Hill College, in Mobile, Alabama but quickly became disillusioned with college life. She failed to complete a full semester before dropping out and moving back to California.

Here she lived with her half-sister in Manhattan Beach and supported herself with a job as a processing clerk.

In 1967 she happened to make acquaintances with Lynette Fromme and Mary Brunner. At this time they were already known as "Charlie's Girls" and wasted no time in introducing the emotionally venerable Krenwinkel to their charismatic leader. Starved for affection and a sense of belonging, 19-year-old Krenwinkel was no match for Charles Manson's charm and charisma. She would later recount how he was the first person to ever call her beautiful, and how he had seduced her on the first night they meeting. The encounter proved to be so emotionally fulfilling for her that she had been unable to stop herself from crying. In just a few days she had become so completely captivated by Manson that she readily agreed to join Fromme and Brunner in following him to San Francisco. Abiding by this decision meant that she left behind her car, apartment, last pay check, and severed all contact with her family.

Now known as Katie, one of the many names she would later go by, she traveled with the ever growing Mason Family across the American west. Her first 18-months with the group was shrouded in a haze of sex, drugs, and a sense of unconditional love. Even now her memories are tarnished with wistful idealism.

"We were just like wood nymphs and wood creatures," she explained in an interview. "We would run through the woods with flowers in our hair, and Charles would have a small flute."

Manson helped promote this delusion of an enchanted life, by exploiting any opportunity to connect himself to people of fame or influence. One such opportunity presented itself in the summer of 1968. While hitchhiking around Los Angeles with fellow Family member, Ella Bailey, Krenwinkel was offered a lift from Dennis Wilson, a drummer and founding member of the Beach Boys. Since he was needed at a recording session, Wilson invited the women to stay at his home in the meantime. It was an offer that would readily be made in the 60s and he thought nothing of it. When he returned later that evening, however, he was startled to find the entire Manson Family on the premises. Without hesitation, they had moved into his home, ate his food, and slept in his bedrooms. Perhaps the most startling moment for Wilson was his first meeting with Manson himself. According to Wilson, Mason greeted him in his driveway and, in a surreal gesture, invited Wilson into his own home. It is a testament to Mason's skills of manipulation that the Family was not immediately removed. Wilson admits that he had at first been fascinated by Manson, his philosophies, and his music. He allowed the family to stay with him until their presence began to create financial problems, and even then it was Wilson's manager that forced them out.

But as they 60's came to an end, people began to lose interest in the hippie movement. 'Free-love' and liberal drug use were no longer as readily acceptable as they once were and people were beginning to return to a more mainstream way of life. Perceiving the threat this posed to the structure and longevity of his Family, Manson resolved that they should now live in isolated from the rest of the world. He found the perfect location Spahn's Ranch. It was nestled in the hills above the San Fernando Valley and, while it was occasionally used by ranch hands, had only one owner. A blind and eighty-year-old man named George Spahn. Manson convinced Spahn to allow his Family, by then consisting of approximately thirteen women, five men, and a number of illegitimate children, to set up residence. In return, the Family, more specifically the Manson women, would care for the property and Spahn's more personal needs. In 1969 they moved into the now infamous ranch and life in the Manson Family took a disturbing turn.

Devoted Lynette "Squeaky" Fromme took on the task of being Spahn's "eyes", but perhaps more accurately, was his de facto wife. Meanwhile, Krenwinkel, while not being the biological mother to any of the children, had been entrusted to be a motherly figure for all Family members. As she attests, it was common practice for anyone uncomfortable with Manson's increasingly disturbing demands, to be sent to her. She would alleviate their concerns and convince them to stay.

At first, the family drew little attention, perhaps because they weren't the first cult to have made the ranch their home. The Fountain of the World, led by Krishna Venta, had resided there from the 1940s to 1950s. It has never been substantiated, but it is believed that Manson had spent time with this cult and that he may have been involved with ex-members who, in 1958, killed Venta and several others in an explosion.

Without prying eyes, Manson tightened his hold on his Family. Aside from mandatory orgies, his favored technique was to initiate numerous acid trips. As Leslie Van Houten, who was convicted alongside Krenwinkel, once explained, "I became saturated in acid and had no sense of where those who were not part of the psychedelic reality came from. I had no perception or sense that I was no longer in control of my mind." During these times Manson would take a far smaller dose, or abstain altogether, to ensure he was the only person to maintain their mental faculties. He used these unguarded moments to gather personal information from Krenwinkel and his other followers, information that he would then use to manipulate them when sober. He also abused their acid trips to push his standing from leader to god. To secure their loyalty and devotion, Manson would re-enact scenes from the crucifixion with himself as Christ. Krenwinkel has described these portrayals as so detailed and bloody that they were "hard to watch". His efforts paid off, however, and his followers no longer saw him as just a talented and wise man, but as the second coming of the messiah.

Around this time Mason began to repeat long, hypnotic, sermons about what he called "Helter Skelter", which he likened to Armageddon. He convinced Krenwinkel and his Family that a race war was inevitable. According to him, the black population would engage the white population in a war that would destroy not just America, but the world as they knew it. The Family would survive because he would lead them to a hole he had found in the desert and keep them safely there until the fighting was over. He asserted that, while the black population would be victorious, they would not be able to govern themselves and would, therefore, look for a white man to lead them. That is when the Family would emerge from their hiding place and race over the desert in their custom-made dune buggies. On this day Manson, and by extension his followers, would become the rulers of whatever population remained on earth. Today Krenwinkel is quick to point out just how foolish, naive, and insane the notion is. But surrounded by her then beloved family on Spahn Ranch, with acid in her veins and Manson's voice in her ear, it seemed completely and unquestionably real.

Mason's vision of the future once again twisted life within the Family. They began to steal cars and strip them to create their dune buggies, guns were collected in mass numbers, and each member learned how to shoot. After their arrest, Krenwinkel, Susan Akins, and Leslie Van Houten all attested that they had even been given lessons on how best to stab someone to inflict as much damage as possible. While Mason still tries to distance himself from the crimes of the Family, Krenwinkel, and the others insist that nothing happened on Spahn ranch without Manson's knowledge and expressed approval. Later, prosecutor Vincent Bugliosi noted how his total control would not have been possible if it wasn't for the isolation of the ranch. "There were no newspapers at Spahn Ranch, no clocks. Cut off from the rest of society, he created in this timeless land a tight little society of his own, with its own value system. It was holistic, complete, and totally at odds with the world outside".

But as the months passed without a hint of an uprising, Mason maintained that he wasn't wrong about Helter Skelter. He began to preach that the delay was because the black population lacked the intelligence to initiate the war on their own, and so it was, therefore, their duty to antagonize the white population themselves. His plan to do this was to frame black men for the murder of rich white people. On Friday, August 9, 1969, after an uneventful dinner, Mason told Susan Atkins, Linda Kasabian, and Patricia Krenwinkle, to leave with fellow member "Tex" Watson in a car borrowed from a ranch hand. The women were ordered to obey Tex's every instructed and, as they were leaving, Mason stopped the car and gave them one last command. "Leave a sign. You girls know what to write."

On this fateful night, no-one at 10050 Cielo Drive had any notion of the danger that was closing in on them. While her husband, Roman Polanski, was in Europe, Actress Sharon Tate was taking advantage of the few months she had left before the birth of their first child. She had invited friends Steven Parent, Wojtek Frykowski, Abigail Folger, and Jay Sebring over to enjoy a quite night in. Parent, still just a teenager, was the first to die. As Kasabian remained as a lookout, the others got around the locked security gate by scaling an embankment. They then climbed a telephone pole to cut the phone lines and began up the dimly lit driveway.

Parent was caught off guard by Tex Watson as he headed to his car. The older man slashed Parent before shooting him four times in the face at close range. They left his body where it fell and entered the home by slicing open one of the fly screens.

Once they were inside they herded the terrified occupants into the living room and Krenwinkel herself dragged Abigail Folger from the bedroom to join the execution line. They momentarily lost control as their victims fought back, and in the resulting chaos, Jay Sebring was shot and the others scattered. Wojciech Frykowski, who managed to get out the front door, was quickly recaptured. His brutal fate included being shot twice, stabbed 51 times, and receiving more than a dozen strikes with the butt of a pistol to his head.

While this was happening Folger, who had already been stabbed, broke away from Krenwinkel and escaped the house. Folger screamed as she ran across the property but Krenwinkel chased her down, pinned her to the ground, and proceeded to stab her repeatedly. The attack was so vicious that, when Folger's body was discovered the next day, her white nightgown was so stained with blood that the police thought it was originally red. According to Krenwinkel, Folger's last words were, "stop, I'm already dead".

After the attack, Krenwinkel returned to the house and got Watson. He followed her to Folger's body and stabbed her himself. "I stabbed her and I kept stabbing her," Krenwinkel later said at her trial. When she was then asked how she felt during the attack she replied, "Nothing, I mean, what is there to describe? It was just there, and it was right."

Meanwhile, the other Family members had shot Jay Sebring in the face and stabbed him several times. Sharon was the last to die. Reportedly, as she had sustained each of the sixteen stab wounds to her back and chest, she had begged that they spare the life of her unborn child. Atkins would later brag that she had told Tate, "I don't care about you or your baby," before delivering the fatal blow. Krenwinkel proceeded to use Tate's blood to fulfill Mason's order to leave a message by writing things such as 'pig' across the walls.

Only one person, caretaker William Garretson, survived the night. He lived in the caretaker's quarters which were separate from the main house. That night, the distance and the loud music he was blaring, ensured that he couldn't hear the attack. Initially, Garretson was a lead suspect and was taken in for questioning. He was late released and police were left baffled by the senseless, brutal crime.

It took a few days for the real horrors to be reviled, but fear gripped Hollywood overnight. Manson didn't wait to send his Family out for another attack. The next night Krenwinkel was once again selected for the task, along with Watson, Atkins, Kasabian, Steve Grogan and Leslie Van Houten. Together with Manson himself, they traveled to the Los Feliz home of grocers Leon and Rosemary LaBianca. However, once he had helped Watson restrain the couple, he once again took measures to distance himself. He directed

Krenwinkel, Van Houten, and Watson to kill the LaBianca's while he left with the others.

This direction was all the trio needed. They obediently carried out his order, holding Mrs. LaBianca in the master bedroom while they tortured and murdered Mr. LaBianca in the living room. Reportedly, as she heard her husband's screams, Mrs. LaBianca had struggled violently. Van Houten held her down while Krenwinkel attempted to stab her with a dull kitchen knife. The blade proved unable to properly break the skin and so the women called for Watson. When he entered the room he was carrying a bayonet the Family had brought to the house with them and proceeded to stab her. According to their later confessions, each member present participated in the repeated stabbing of Mrs. LaBianca.

There is some dispute over who carved the word 'war' onto Leon LaBianca's abdomen. In his book, Will You Die for Me? Watson took responsibility for the macabre act. Be this as it may, many still attribute the act to Krenwinkel. Watson further maintains that, as he washing the blood off of himself, Krenwinkel repeatedly stabbed the already dead Mr. LaBianca with a carving fork, which she left in his abdomen. Krenwinkel admits that she did stab LaBianca, but asserts that it was at Watson's insistence since Manson had instructed that everyone present had to partake in each kill.

Krenwinkel once again used their victim's blood to write their messages, including 'death to pigs' on the walls, and 'helter skelter' on the refrigerator. In no hurry to leave the trio ate and showered within the LaBianca home.

Additionally, they also spent time playing with the LaBianca's two dogs before hitchhiking back to the Spahn Ranch. When questioned about this night Krenwinkel will later claim that her only thought during the murders was, "Now he won't be sending any of his children off to war." While the trio carried out his bidding, Mason, Atkins, Grogan, and Kasabian prowled Los Angeles in search for another victim. As perhaps the only mercy of this night they were unable to find one.

The murders forever altered Los Angeles. In the words of one long-term resident, "after the second murders, the gates went up all over the city". Even the Family wasn't left untouched by paranoia and fear. As the police chased down each possible lead, some within the Family had become suspicious of their own. Rumours began to circle Krenwinkel and the others involved and many began to question Manson's teachings.

The breaking point came for many when, a week after the murders, the Los Angeles County Sheriff's Department arrested Manson, Krenwinkel, and a few other Family members. They were not arrested on homicide, however, but due to an unrelated investigation involving stolen cars that were spotted in and around the ranch. In their absence rumors began to circulate through the Family that Donald "Shorty" Shea, a ranch hand that they knew personally, had been murdered by someone within their ranks. Manson and the others were released when a minor error rendered the search warrant invalid. They quickly returned to the ranch but the damage had already been done.

The Family began to rapidly lose once loyal members and their departures made others question Mason and what they had become involved in. Krenwinkel, however, remained completely dedicated to Manson and a devoted follower of his philosophy. But the raid and subsequent departures had unnerved Manson and he decided to relocate the Family in an attempt to regain control and privacy. Krenwinkel followed him to Baker Ranch near Death Valley and helped to continue the work converting stole cars into dune buggies in preparation for Helter Skelter.

This time, it only took a few months for the authorities to become suspicious. On October 10, 1969, while Manson was elsewhere, the Family was once again raided. A few members, including Krenwinkel, were arrested. This time, however, Krenwinkel's estranged father arrived and posted her bail. Unable to understand or compete with Mason's hold, he failed to keep her from returning to the ranch.

When she arrived, Manson, who suspected the police were closing in, instantly sent her away to stay with her mother in Alabama. He told her that she mustn't return until he sent orders for her to do so. He was arrested on Barker Ranch two days later. Despite the best efforts of local law enforcement, the final unraveling of the Mason Family came from an unlikely source. Susan Atkins, proud of her involvement in both the Tate and LaBianca murders and desperate to brag, had thought her cellmate Veronica

"Ronnie" Howard would keep her secret. Instead, she instantly told the authorities. Armed with both Akins' confession and Howard's statement, the police arrested Krenwinkel near her aunt's house in Mobile, Alabama on December 1, 1969. The next day Krenwinkel was indicted for seven counts of first-degree murder and one count of conspiracy to commit murder.

Desperate to fight her extradition to California, Krenwinkel's lawyers asserted that she had only fled to Alabama because she believed Manson would attempt to kill her. In February 1970, as Van Houten, Atkins, and Mason were set to stand trial, Krenwinkel received a letter from Manson. He asked her to join him and the others so that they can put together a united defense. Immediately, despite the protests of her lawyers, she contacted the district attorney of Mobile and stated her wish to sign the extradition and return to California as so as possible. She fired her lawyers and voluntarily returned to California and her Family. For his part, Watson didn't follow suit and fought extradition from his home state of Texas until the end. He was unsuccessful, but the legal process took long enough to ensure that he was tried separately.

The trial of the Manson Family captivated the world. Not just because the horror of the crimes, nor the fame of the victims, but because of the obsessional loyalty that they family continued to show Manson and each other. Free members staged sit-ins outside of the courthouse for the months of the trial and preached to anyone who would listen that Mason had only taught them unconditional love and peace.

Paul Fitzgerald, a lawyer from the public defender's office, offered his services to Frenwinkel and the other 'Manson Girls'. Working on a pro-bono basis the case almost ruined him financially and he faced a battle on all fronts. Not only was there insurmountable evidence against them, and the girl's in-court antics ruined any presumption of innocence that the jury might have held, but he was unable to stem the influence that Charles Manson wielded over his clients.

Of all the lawyers that were hired to represent the trio's defense, few besides Fitzgerald had any real trial experience and none had ever worked a murder case before. Every time it was suggested that the women be tried separately, or that Mason could have even been remotely responsible, the lawyer proposing the argument would be fired. Mason would then hire another, more incompetent and ill prepared, lawyer to represent the girls instead. He would order the girls to confess and say that he was in no way involved. He would instruct Krenwinkel, Atkins, and Van Houten to mark their foreheads in the same manner he did, shave their heads in a sign of solidarity, and disrupt the proceedings of their trial by spontaneously chanting insults and nonsense he selected. By all accounts, Fitzgerald believed that Manson cared less about securing his freedom than he did about maintaining his hold on the minds of these three women.

Over the nine-month trial, Krenwinkel, Atkins, and Van Houten often wore multi-coloured mini dresses that the other Family women had stolen for them, came to court barefoot, and constantly changed their appearance to match Manson. Most of the time they seemed disconnected from reality and unaware of the gravity of their situation. They would skip to and from the courtroom, hold hands, and sing songs Manson had written. They would spend their time doodling pictures of demons and satanic symbols. One of the few times they were interested in the trail was when former Family member Linda Kasabian took the witness stand. Having made a deal for leniency, Kasabian became a star witness for the prosecution. Krenwinkel and the others attempted to intimidate her each time she took the stand by copying her looks, such as matching their hairstyles to hers, and unnervingly staring.

Throughout the trial, Krenwinkel's parents made several attempts to connect with their daughter but were rebuffed each time. Her father described her as having a different personality and this is a sentiment that Krenwinkel herself would later echo. In a recent interview, she said that "at the trial, I had given up every little part of me to a man that demanded every little part of me".

With all the hindrances placed upon him, Fitzgerald could barely mount a reasonable defense. He could do little but argue that Krenwinkel's fingerprints, found in the Tate house, might not have been there from the night of the murder. That perhaps, at another time, she had been "an invited guest or friend". The jury did not agree and, on March 29, 1971, Manson, Krenwinkel, Atkins, and Van Houten were all found guilty of first-degree murder. They were subsequently sentenced to death and the women were transferred to the California Institution for Women (CIW) near Corona, California.

Once again the social changes of the time worked in Manson's favor. During the time of their trial the California Supreme Court was hearing the case of People v. Anderson, to determine if the state of California would abolish the death plenty. It struck many as ironic or unjust that since it was determined that the death plenty was "cruel and unusual" punishment, Manson and his followers would receive the mercy they never offered their victims. Their death sentences were automatically commuted to life in prison.

As she began her life sentence, Krenwinkel remained fiercely loyal to Manson and the Family. When now asked to explain this connection she offers that she might have held onto it because the other choice was admitting that "everything I had believed in was now wrong", and that, without this bond, she would have to confront the fact that she was "fully responsible for the damage, the wreckage, and the horror," that she had created.

Time and distance efficiently worked to erode Mason's hold. After the arduous journey of evaluating who she had become, Krenwinkel, by all accounts, confront her actions and accepted responsibility for them. In so doing she has transformed herself into a model inmate. She has maintained a perfect prison record and is active within prison programs such as Alcoholics Anonymous and Narcotics Anonymous. She teaches illiterate prisoners how to read and participates in the prison volleyball and softball teams. Her development has also been of a personal nature. She now writes both poetry and music, plays the guitar, and has earned a Bachelor's degree in Human Services from the University of La Verne.

The accomplishment she is most proud of, however, is that she is now her own person. "I am who I am today because I fought desperately for it," she said in an interview. As she explained, she can now be certain that each belief, notion, and preference she has is truly her own. Instead of blind obedience, she questions, debates, evaluates and comes to her own conclusions. "I learned choice at a horrific cost".

While all of them have been eligible for parole, only Watson, who was convicted after Manson and the women, has been released back into the general public. Mason remains at Corcoran State Prison, just north of Los Angeles, and in 2007 was denied parole for the 11th time. He no longer has the all-consuming hold he once had, but he still manages to wield public interest and insists on his innocence. He maintains that he had never told Krenwinkel nor anyone else to do anything. According to him, ever decision they made was their own, and in no way included him.

Krenwinkel is still incarcerated in the California Institution for Women in Chino, California. At her parole hearing in 2004, she was asked who she would place at the top of the list for people she has harmed. "Myself," was her response. She was denied parole since, according to the panel, she still posed an "unacceptable risk to public safety". In total, she has been denied parole thirteen times, the last time in January 2011. Each time the panel is swayed by the memory of the crimes and, at the last parole hearing, the 80 letters from all over the world urging them to keep her incarcerated.

Diane Sawyer interviewed Krenwinkel in 1994 and found her honestly remorseful. According to the interview, the victim that haunts her the most is Folger. As she stated to Sawyer, "That was just a young women that I killed, who had parents. She was supposed to live a life and her parents were never supposed to see her dead." She also spoke to Sawyer about her feelings of responsibility and guilt. "I wake up every day knowing that I'm a destroyer of the most precious thing, which is life; and I do that because that is what I deserve, to wake up every morning and know that." Also, during the same interview, she demonstrated that the considerable hold Manson had once had on her was truly severed. In an act that would have been inconceivable during the trial, she asserted that Mason was "absolutely lying" about not ordering the murders. And that nothing would have happened without his direct influence.

In 2009, Susan Akin's, who had also had an exemplary prison record and believed that she had experienced a religious awakening, died of brain cancer. She was 61.

Krenwinkel still maintains a close relationship with Leslie Van Houten, who has also expressed remorse and responsibility. Having stated that "being a follower does not excuse", Van Houten has earned a degree, writes short stories, and advocates for the homeless. While many raise questions about the girl's ongoing connection, they argue that no one else would ever be able to understand what it was like to be part of the Family, how hard it was to break away, and difficult it is to live with the consequences. Perhaps it is this support that allowed Krenwinkel, in an interview with filmmaker Olivia Klaus for the documentary, My Life After Manson, to admit that she was a "coward". And that it was this cowardice that led her to not just join the Family, but was also the reason she committed the "horrendous" and "abominable" acts.

Very little remains of the Spahn Ranch. Spahn himself has moved on and the structures that were left behind were destroyed in a fire. Numerous owners have attempted to shake off the history of the land and create something new, but each has failed. Now owned by the state, the property has been left for the elements to claim with no attempt at upkeep. Every so often the ranch would receive tourists of the macabre and, with the rise of paranormal-themed television shows, has been visited by ghost hunters. But there is very little proof that the Manson Family had ever been there. By the creek where they had practiced shooting there is a tree with a rusted chain and a hunk of metal that may have once been a sink. One of the most infamous photographs taken of the Manson Family had been within a cave on the property. Now it stands, littered with beer cans, with a small boulder marking the site. Etched into that stone is a simple sentence that, at one time, would have been benign and forgettable, but now brings to mind madness, murder, and the dozens of innocent lives that were destroyed by one man's pursuit of control and the promise of love.

CLARA SCHWARTZ

The story of Clara Schwartz is one of a troubled young woman who had a turbulent relationship with her father. While this is certainly not an unusual situation, the outcome, in the case, was deadly. In December of 2001, Schwartz enlisted the help of friends, including a mentally ill teenager, to murder her father Robert Schwartz. Through an elaborate and twisted role-playing game, Schwartz turned a few misfits into a band of loyal followers who would kill for her.

Schwartz had met Kyle Hulbert at a Renaissance fair in the fall of the same year. She told Hulbert horror stories about her father, claiming he abused her and that she feared he would soon try to poison her. Hulbert, who had a long history of mental illness, believed Schwartz without question. Schwartz invited Hulbert to take part in a role-playing game she had invented called Underworld.

Through this game, Schwartz used her character to convince Hulbert's character, an assassin, to kill her father. Sometime between when the game began and December of 2001, it became clear that Schwartz wanted her father dead in real life. Hulbert, all too willing to do whatever Schwartz said, agreed.

Hulbert, accompanied by two mutual friends of his and Schwartz's who were in on the game, drove to the country home of Robert Schwartz on December 8, 2001. He used a samurai sword to stab Robert over and over, leaving him for dead. It was only through the carelessness of Hulbert and his accomplices that the story of Schwartz and the deadly game she orchestrated came to light.

Early Life

Clara Schwartz was born in 1981 to Robert Schwartz and his wife. Clara was the youngest of the Schwartz's three children, which included herself, an older sister Catherine, and her older brother Jesse. Robert Scwhartz was a well-known researcher and scientist. He worked in the field of biometrics and DNA research, gaining national recognition for his work. Robert was also a founding member of the Virginia Biotechnology Association.

Despite her father's successful career, Clara Schwartz was closer to her mother than her father. In fact, her relationship with her father Robert was strained for her whole life. The two argued frequently and never got along.

When Clara Schwartz was just a teenager, around the age of fifteen, her mother became sick with cancer and eventually passed away. After this tragedy, Clara withdrew even further from her father and her peers. She became a loner and dressed in the "goth" style, associating only with friends who were also part of the goth subculture. Clara listened to heavy metal music and enjoyed playing fantasy roleplaying games, which offered an escape from reality. It was this tendency to involve herself in an alternative circle of friends with unusual interests that ultimately helped Schwartz orchestrate her father's murder.

The Crime

Previous Attempts

Clara Schwartz had been planning to kill her father for some time. During her murder trial, Schwartz's former boyfriend Patrick House testified about Schwartz's intentions dating back to before she had even met Kyle Hulbert, the man who would ultimately murder her father.

House stated that while he had been dating Schwartz, she often spoke about killing her father. She researched herbal poisons, saying that she wanted it to appear that her father died of natural causes. House also said that Schwartz discussed with him how much money she would inherit if her father were dead, and she was concerned that her father was going to cut her out of his will due to their rocky relationship.

Schwartz had also involved House in a roleplaying game she invented called Underworld. In this game, Clara called herself the "Lord of Chaos". House's character was an assassin. Schwartz began with roleplaying, asking House to kill her father in character. House, in his roleplaying character, agreed.

However, it progressed beyond simple roleplay. Schwartz began asking House when he was really going to kill her father. House became uneasy and ended things between the two of them.

Schwartz and Hulbert Meet

It was the fall of 2001 when Clara Schwartz and Kyle Hulbert met at a renaissance fair. Hulbert was a very troubled young man. Though he was only eighteen years old when he met Schwartz, Hulbert had already been placed in mental institutions seven different times in the past twelve years.

Hulbert had several diagnoses of mental illness already as well. He suffered from both bipolar disorder and schizophrenia. Schizophrenia blurred the lines between fantasy and reality in Hulbert's mind, while bipolar disorder made him subject to fits of rage and aggressive behavior. Hulbert had just been released after his latest stay in a psychiatric facility four months before meeting Schwartz.

Schwartz was nineteen years old and a student at James Madison University when she and Hulbert met. Though she was now in college, Schwartz and her father continued to have a rocky relationship. Schwartz was also heavily involved in goth subculture. She and Hulbert shared an interest in the occult, magic, and fantasy.

Schwartz introduced Hulbert to the roleplaying game she had invented called Underworld. Her friends Katherine Inglis and Michael Pfohl were also part of the game, acting as Schwartz's loyal followers. In this fantasy world they created, Schwartz was known as the Priestess of High Chaos. Hulbert became a warrior and Schwartz's protector in the game. The two formed a very close bond.

Lead-up to the Murder

In instant messages and emails police found between Schwartz, Inglis, Pfohl, and Hulbert, Schwartz's fantasy world becomes clear. Schwartz used coded messages, blurring the lines between the game and her real life. In these cryptic messages, she refers to her father as "Old Guy" or "OG" and instead of the word murder uses the code word "tay".

In exchanges between Schwartz and her band of followers, Schwartz described her father as abusive. She claimed that he hit her, pulled her hair, and told her how he disapproved of her friends and her lifestyle. Schwartz even said that she believed her father was trying to poison her. This account is disputed by Schwartz's two siblings, both of whom testified against her during the murder trial and stated that their father had never been abusive.

Before the night of the murder, Hulbert had met Robert Schwartz several times. On one occasion, Clara Schwartz had handed Hulbert a piece of cooked pork that her father had made, claiming it was poisoned. Hulbert tasted it, and in his later written confession to police stated, "I could tell it had been tampered with, both by taste and by smell."

On another visit, Hulbert saw Schwartz's father serving her pork chops and lemon. Hulbert became convinced, with encouragement from Schwartz, that her father was poisoning her food, specifically the pork chops and lemon.

In the month before the murder, Schwartz and Hulbert's communications became more intense and more directly hinted at the possibility of Hulbert murdering Robert. On November 9, 2001, in an instant message sent to Schwartz, Hulbert asked, "If I was to tay him would you be mad at me?" "Tay" was their secret code word for "kill"—Hulbert was clearly asking Schwartz if he should kill her father.

Schwartz replied, "No. Just don't do it now."

Hulbert continued, asking, "Maybe in a month?"

Schwartz deflected and told Hulbert she didn't want to discuss it online. Instead, she said, "We'll talk about it down here. Take a long walk and talk. I just hate talking about that kind of stuff on here." However, Hulbert's suggestion that he commit the murder in a month must have been well-received by Schwartz, as it was nearly exactly one month later that he killed Robert Schwartz.

The two continued to talk about the possibility of Hulbert killing Schwartz's father through email and instant messages. In another online conversation, Schwartz told Hulbert that if he was to kill her father, "all I ask is that it not trace to me."

Throughout the month of November 2001, Schwartz continued to hint at the possibility of Hulbert killing her father. She told him how her life would be better without her father around and speculated about what it would be like if her father was dead. During this time, Hulbert came to believe that Schwartz's father was going to kill her on an upcoming trip to the Virgin Islands.

At the end of November, Schwartz sent Hulbert $60 via overnight mail. It was later revealed that she intended for Hulbert to use this money to purchase gloves and a do-rag to avoid leaving behind any evidence such as DNA, fingerprints, or strands of hair. With her father's work as an expert in DNA and biotechnology, Schwartz would have been very familiar with the concept of DNA evidence and wanted to be cautious. Schwartz also wanted Hulbert to use the money to buy the gas he would need to drive to her father's house.

The Murder

On the night of December 8, 2001, Kyle Hulbert, Katherine Inglis, and Michael Pfohl got into a car and drove to Robert Schwartz's farm house in Loudon, Virginia. It was a cold, rainy Saturday night. Clara Schwartz was in her dorm room at James Madison University.

Inglis and Pfohl dropped Hulbert off at Robert's house and waited. Hulbert had a 27-inch samurai sword hidden on his person. He knocked on the front door and Robert answered. Hulbert asked if Schwartz was home, and Robert told him she was not. Hulbert asked to come in and get Clara's number.

Robert let Hulbert into his home, a fatal mistake. Hulbert used his bathroom, then followed Robert into the dining room. Here, Hulbert began asking about Robert's alleged abuse of his daughter. He demanded to know if Robert was hurting Schwartz and if he was planning to kill her. Hulbert claimed he told Robert, "I know about your plans. You won't get away with it."

According to Hulbert, Robert had a guilty look in his eyes. To Hulbert, this was proof that Robert was abusing his daughter. Hulbert claimed that Robert smiled at him and smacked him in the face. Hulbert took out the sword and began slashing at Robert.

The attack brought Robert to his knees, where he began pleading and trying to defend himself. Hulbert then stabbed Robert. He claimed that Robert smiled at him, and this infuriated Hulbert. He went into a fit of rage, stabbing Hulbert over and over. According to Hulbert's later written confession, Robert looked up at him and asked "What did I ever do to you?" Hulbert stabbed him one final time after this and killed him.

After the attack, Hulbert rinsed off his sword. He turned off the lights in Robert's home, then left quickly. Hulbert later stated that he heard voices in his head telling him he had to get out fast, because Robert's soul had already left his body.

Aftermath of the Murder

Hulbert went back outside to the car and handed the sword to Pfohl. Pfohl wiped the sword with a towel, wrapped it up, and stashed it in the back of the car. However, the group had encountered a problem. The rain had turned the dirt to mud, and their car was stuck.

Inglis claimed that she asked Hulbert to go back inside and borrow Robert Schwartz's phone to call a tow truck. According to her testimony, Hulbert told her and Pfohl that nobody was home, but she suspected Hulbert had killed Robert. Instead, the group used a neighbor's phone to call for a tow truck. Later, this allowed police to easily identify Schwartz's co-conspirators.

The murder of Robert Schwartz wasn't discovered until the following Monday when Schwartz didn't show up to work. Police went to his home and found the scene of the bloody murder. They immediately began investigating Robert's family and looking at Clara Schwartz.

Police pulled phone records from Schwartz's dorm room and found that she had received a phone call right after the murder. Schwartz tried to lie, saying she did not receive any phone calls. When police showed the evidence of the call, Schwartz began blaming Hulbert, saying it was his idea to kill her father.

On December 11, Inglis, Pfohl, and Hulbert were arrested and questioned. Inglis was the first to agree to speak to the police. She minimized her own role in the crime. According to her version of events, she and Pfohl dropped Hulbert off with no direct knowledge of his plans. Inglis claimed that Hulbert told them he was going to do a job or a favor for Schwartz. She also claimed that it wasn't until Hulbert returned with the bloody sword that she suspected he had killed Robert, though she still wasn't certain and didn't act on this suspicion.

The Trial

Inglis' confession brought the entire conspiracy to light. She made a plea bargain with police, and in the end served only a year in jail for her part in the murder of Robert Schwartz. Pfohl confessed as well, pleading to second degree murder. His family made statements asking for lenience, saying the Pfohl was suicidal and easily swayed by Schwartz, wanting to fit in with her group. Pfohl was sentenced to eighteen years in prison.

Hulbert gave a written statement to police, confessing to his crime, but he was not scheduled to have his own trial until after Schwartz.

Clara Schwartz was the only one of the group who ended up going trial. Even before the trial began, Schwartz's own family was against her. Nearly all of her relatives, including her brother and sister, signed a letter asking the judge to keep Schwartz in jail prior to and during the trial. They agreed that she was a danger to herself and others.

The trial took place in October of 2002, less than a year after the murder. Her attorneys argued that she had no real connection to the murder. Instead, they said, this was the result of a misunderstanding between Schwartz and Hulbert. They argued that Schwartz had believed their conversations about murdering her father were all part of their roleplaying game. There was no way, they said, that she could have known Hulbert was going to act on their plot in the real world.

The prosecution had a star witness, however. Schwartz's former boyfriend, Patrick House, came to testify against her. House told how Schwartz had tried to convince him to murder her father before, using the same manipulative techniques based on her roleplaying game. In addition to House's testimony, Schwartz's friend and co-conspirator Inglis testified against her. Inglis described how Schwartz had talked about her father's abuse, provoking Hulbert to commit the murder.

Members of Schwartz's own family testified against her. They argued that she was never abused by her father, painting a picture of a troubled young woman who simply never got along with her father and was interested in the money she might inherit if he died.

On October 15, 2002, after a short one week trial and four hours of deliberation by the jury, Schwartz was found guilty. The jury recommended a sentence of 48 years.

Schwartz's attorneys tried to fight this long sentence recommendation. They argued that the jury had not taken long enough to consider the evidence in full. They also attempted to make the case again during sentencing hearings in February that Schwartz had been abused by her father. Schwartz's defense team claimed that the prosecution had withheld evidence proving that Schwartz was abused.

During this time, the testimony of one of Schwartz's old high school teachers came to light as well. The teacher stated that Schwartz's father had verbally abused her. Schwartz's family admitted that Schwartz and her father often got into intense arguments, but that there was no abuse in the home.

Finally, the defense attempted to argue that Schwartz suffered from hyperthyroidism, a condition that they claimed inhibited her ability to think clearly and logically. One of Schwartz's uncles, the only family member who testified on her behalf during the entire trial, supported this theory. He backed up the defense's claim that Schwartz was a troubled girl whose mind was clouded by hyperthyroidism, causing her not to realize that she was driving Hulbert to murder her father.

The judge dismissed all of these concerns and upheld the original sentence of 48 years in prison.

Hulbert's Confession

Kyle Hulbert had already given a written statement to police confessing to his involvement in the murder of Robert Schwartz. He had no choice but to either admit guilt in court and accept his punishment or to plead insanity.

Despite a lengthy history of mental illness, Hulbert and his attorneys chose not to pursue an insanity plea. Due to the fact that Hulbert had clearly planned out the crime, an insanity plea was unlikely to work—clearly, he was sane enough to plot a murder.

At a hearing on March 10, 2003, Hulbert confessed to the crime in court. He said he believed it was the right thing to do and would spare the Schwartz family from the agony of another trial connected to the case. Hulbert admitted to feeling guilty, saying he wished he had never met Schwartz and that she had manipulated him into murdering her father.

A psychiatrist testified that Hulbert had many imaginary friends and was seeking a sense of belonging. The psychiatrist claimed that Schwartz gave Hulbert that sense of family and thus manipulated him into doing her bidding.

In the end, Hulbert was given a life sentence for the murder of Robert Schwartz. Ten years were added to the sentence for conspiracy charges as well, ensuring that Hulbert will remain in prison for his entire life.

Although all testimony and evidence pointed to Clara Schwartz as the mastermind behind her father's murder, all those involved suffered the consequences of their actions. Schwartz's ability to manipulate her peers, especially those who already felt rejected by society, was the real deadly force in this case. Without her loyal followers, Schwartz never could have committed the horrific murder of her father.

Jonestown

Dorothy Miller

139

Jim Jones, leader of the "Peoples Temple"

This is the man that we all think of when we hear the words the "Peoples Temple," "cult leader," "mass murderer" and, of course, "Don't drink the Kool-Aid." To this day, people wonder how Jim Jones evolved from an idealistic young man to a maniacal cult leader who led a mass suicide in the country of Guyana.

Early Life

James Warren Jones was born on May 13, 1931, in Crete, Indiana. His father, James Thurman Jones, was a disabled World War I veteran with an alcohol problem who later found work as a mystic fortune teller. His mother, Lynetta, was no stranger to the occult world herself as she believed that her newborn son would become a messiah.

During the Great Depression when finding jobs was difficult enough without the added alcoholism and being a "mystic fortune teller," the Jones' were forced to move to the town of Lynn, Indiana where they lived in a shack with no plumbing. Jones was considered a strange child who found more interest in reading books about leaders from history like Stalin, Marx, Gandhi, and Hitler. He studied the teachings of these men carefully, learning their strength and weaknesses, wanting to mimic their success in leading people.

A solitary youth, Jim was befriended by a neighbor who took him to church. The ten-year old Jones became enamored with the worship services and began visiting other churches. He would befriend a minister of the local Pentecostal church who inspired him to begin preaching to other children in the community. Young Jim had a difficult time making friends, partially due to his practice of preaching to the kids, but he also disliked what were the typical activities of the teenage boy. He thought sports, drinking, and dancing were all sinful activities. Those that knew him during his childhood would later say that he was obsessed with religion and death. He would hold funerals for animals on his parent's property and one occasion it was alleged that he stabbed a cat to death.

Jones' father was no help throughout his awkward early years. There are suggestions that his father had a connection with the Ku Klux Klan but this was only hearsay. When his father refused to allow one of Jones' black friends into the house, it led to a fight between the two that lasted for many years.

Jones' parents would separate in 1948 and Jones moved with his mother to Richmond, Indiana. He would finish high school there, graduated with honors that same year.

In 1949, Jones married Marceline Baldwin, a nurse four years his senior. They would move to Bloomington where he attended the University of Indiana. It was there where he would hear Eleanor Roosevelt speak on the problems affecting the black community which peaked his interest in civil rights. In 1951, the couple moved to Indianapolis where Jones continued his education at Butler University, earning a degree in secondary education.

Marxism and the Roots of his Religious Career

Beginning in 1951, Jones started going to Communist Party USA gatherings in Indianapolis. He had studied the writings of Karl Marx as a young man when he lived in Lynn, but his actual involvement with the Communist Party did not begin until the 50s when three things happened which changed his views:

◇ Jones and his mother attended an event where the speaker was Paul Robeson, an American bass singer, Rutgers College scholarship winner, class valedictorian, and a person who was very involved with the civil rights movement. This event led to Jones' mother being harassed by the FBI in front of her co-workers.

◇ Jones himself became a target of the McCarthy Hearings due to the event. Jones expressed his frustration at the treatment of those who were open supporters of communists in the United States.

◇ This led Jones to ask himself a defining question which would impact his life. "How can I demonstrate my Marxism and my support of the communist party?" To Jones, the answer was simple. The church.

Church beginnings

A Methodist superintendent who knew that Jones was a communist helped get Jones his beginnings in the church. In 1952, Jones entered the Somerset Southside Methodist Church as a student pastor where he witnessed the wealthier people being more attracted to faith healing. He then decided to incorporate this into his 'act'.

Later, Jones would claim that he left the Somerset Southside Methodist Church due to the church banning him from allowing blacks to attend his services. He attended a faith-healing at a Seventh Day Adventist Church which is when he realized that he needed religion to gain the money and power to accomplish his social goals which, one would assume from his dedication to Marxism, was to infiltrate the church and convert the followers to communism.

Between June 11th to June 15th of 1956, Jones held a religious convention with the Reverend William M. Branham, an evangelist who was as well-known then as Oral Robert was in the 1980s. After the convention was over, Jones was able to launch his own church, which would be known as the Peoples Temple Christian Church Full Gospel. His church would have no restrictions on race and all people were welcome – a rather progressive concept for the year 1956.

In 1960, Jones was appointed as the director of the *Human Rights Commission* by Indianapolis Mayor Charles Boswell. Although he had been asked by Boswell to maintain a low profile, he would not or could not, and would publicly speak on local radio and television. The mayor and commissioners again asked Jones to tone it down a bit, and he responded by cheering loudly at a meeting of the NAACP and Urban League where he urged the audience to be even more militant, even ending the speech with "Let my people go!"

During this same time Jones fought for the integration of many public institutions in Indiana, such as police stations, hospitals, churches, restaurants, the Methodist Hospital, and an amusement park. He went as far as to set up sting operations in which he would catch businesses refusing to serve black customers and would then write the leaders of the *American Nazi Party* and publicly leak the responses to the media. He faced much scrutiny and criticism for his actions and views on integration of the races. At different times during this period, a swastika was drawn on the Temple, the corpse of a cat was thrown at his house, dynamite was left in a coal pile near the Temple, and the family and Temple received harassing and threatening letters.

The Rainbow Family

As if to further his determination regarding equality for all races, Jim and Marceline then adopted three children that were at least partially non-Caucasian, which Jones referred to as his "rainbow family." He was quoted as saying "Integration is a more personal thing with me now. It's a question of my son's future" although he also portrayed the Temple itself as a "rainbow family." Three of his children, Lew, Suzanne, and Stephanie, were of Korean-American ancestry as Jones had been encouraging his supporters to adopt from Korea where the war was on-going and devastating both the country and the people. In 1954, they adopted Agnes, an 11-year-old partially Native American. Suzanne, one of the Korean-American children, was adopted in 1959 when she was six years old. In June of 1959, Marceline would give birth do their only biological child. They named the baby Stephan Gandhi Jones.

In 1961, they adopted James Warren Jones, Jr., becoming the first Caucasian couple in the state of Indiana to adopt a black child. They also adopted Timothy Glen Tupper, a son of a member of the temple.

The Peoples Temple goes to Brazil

In 1961, Jones gave a speech what he saw as the impending nuclear attack on America and decided that it was time for him, his immediate family, the "rainbow family," and the Peoples Temple to leave America for an area that would be safer when the apocalypse occurred. When *Esquire* magazine ran an article in the January 1962 issue which suggested Belo Horizonte, Brazil as a safe place in case of a nuclear war Jim Jones made plans to relocate to establish a new Temple location. On his way to Brazil, Jones stopped in Guyana for the first time.

In Belo Horizonte, they rented a three-bedroom house where Jones went out to explore and meet the neighbors. He wanted to see if they were receptive to his Marxist ideals but was careful not to reveal that he was a communist himself. He studied the economy and the racial situation in Brazil while trying to decide if this could be another potential location. He found the language barrier to be a difficulty in spreading his message, but it was ultimately the fact that those living in Belo Horizonte did not have the money or the resources to help Jones which caused him to relocate to Rio de Janeiro in mid-1963.

During the time spent in Rio de Janeiro, Jones and the other members of the Peoples Temple worked with the poor in the slums of the city. Jones received messages from those back in Indiana informing him of the civil rights movement and the very real possibility that they were losing any progress that Jones had helped to make in the state. This concerned him and weighed on his mind heavily and helped him decide to relocate back to America, this time to California.

The Return to America

Upon returning from Brazil in 1962 Jones went back to his church in Indiana telling his congregation that on July 15, 1967 a nuclear war would destroy Earth and a new socialist Eden would replace the existing Earth. To survive the nuclear war the family would have to relocate to Northern California, near the city of Ukiah. More than 100 people followed Jones to California and by the 1970s they expanded, opening branches in San Francisco, Los Angeles, and San Fernando. Although the Temple still considered the Redwood Valley branch the "mother church," Jones knew that to grow he needed to move to a more urban area.

In 1971, the Peoples Temple moved their headquarters to San Francisco in the building on Geary Boulevard. San Francisco was the center of protests at the time. The tension in the city gave Jones more exposure and, ultimately, more members. Jones was an impressive speaker. His passion for religion as well as the "healings" only increased both the number of people who fell for his talk of a better life and the amount of money that went into Jones' pockets. Although Jones spoke against sex and romantic relationships, he was known to have several adulterous relationships, one of which resulted in the birth of a son with a church administrator. Jones claimed that he was the father of Grace Stoen's son as well. Although this may have been because he wanted to end all familial bonds and be looked upon as the father of his followers.

The move to the city also allowed Jones to become involved in the political scene in San Francisco. Jones helped get George Moscone elected as the Mayor of San Francisco who then appointed Jones as the Chairman of the San Francisco Housing Authority Commission. His position as the Chairman of the Commission may have been largely in name only, but he did lead the fight against the eviction of poor people in the famous International Hotel by the Four Seas Corporation. This position allowed Jones to meet with influential and well-known figures in the 1970s political arena, including Walter Mondale who publicly praised the Temple, First Lady Rosalynn Carter, who not only corresponded with Jones about Cuba but also spoke at the grand opening of the San Francisco headquarters.

The Los Angeles branch had a mostly African-American following. Many of them moved to San Francisco to be at the headquarters and nearer to Jones himself. In 1974, Jones leased over 3,800 acres of land 150 miles west of the capital of Guyana, Georgetown, to develop into a land for himself and his followers. By this point, Jones had abandoned the idea of making the Redwood Valley location a "promised land" and had decided that Guyana was a better option.

In September of 1977, assemblyman Willie Brown served as the master of ceremonies at a dinner held for Jones that was attended by then Governor Jerry Brown as well as Lieutenant Governor Mervyn Dymally. Governor Brown likened Jones to Martin Luther King, Albert Einstein and and Chairman Mao.

Jones had made many influential friends since the move to San Francisco, but Jones had some controversial opinions that he could not keep to himself such as his admiration for the Symbionese Liberation Army, the Black Panthers, the New World Liberation Front, and the Black Liberation Army. He was not a supporter of the Nation of Islam, considering them to be both sexist and racist, and he was afraid that there would be clashes between the two groups because of their locations in San Francisco. Jones even went as far as to claim that the Nation of Islam had set a fire at the Temple in San Francisco. The relationship between the two groups improved when they held a "Spiritual Jubilee" in Los Angeles in 1976 which drew thousands, including Lieutenant Governor Mervyn Dymally, and the Mayor of Los Angeles, Tom Bradley.

Criticism against the Peoples Temple

Bob Houston and Joyce Shaw were married members of the Temple and owned at house that was used as a communal living facility. Houston questioned Jones about some of his theories and as a result was involved in two of the "boxing matches" held by the Temple which left him beaten. Joyce left the group in July of 1976 and left for Ohio but she called Bob, who was still in the Temple, in October asking him to join her. On the 5th of October, Bob Houston was found dead along some railroad tracks. Bob was the son of Sammy Houston, a photographer for the Associated Press. Sammy was convinced that the Temple was behind the death of his son. When Joyce went to get Bob's personal belongings she was told not to attempt to get Bob's two daughters to leave the Temple as Bob and Joyce had signed documents that they had molested the girls, something that the Temple often required members to do. When Sammy told the Associated Press what was going on the two girls began writing Sammy from Guyana. Sammy told his friend, Congressman Leo Ryan, about the Temple and it was Congressman Ryan who led the investigation into Jonestown in 1978.

In 1972, Grace Stoen gave birth to a son, John. Jones had Timothy Stoen, Grace's husband, sign paperwork that stated that he had encouraged Jones and Grace to have sexual relations which resulted in the birth John, although the birth certificate listed Grace and Timothy as John's parents. Grace did not like the idea of raising John communally and seeing other members of the Temple assaulted only served to strengthen her desire to leave Jones' group. She left the San

Francisco Temple in July 1976 while her son, John, was sent to Guyana. Tim quit his job as Assistant District Attorney and moved to Guyana under Jones' orders. Later, Tim would disappear from the Georgetown, Guyana headquarters. The Stoen's would later form the group "Concerned Relatives" which would lead to the arrival of Congressman Leo Ryan in Guyana.

Before the move to Guyana, Jones would often entertain people of importance at the Temple, including a columnist at the San Francisco Chronicle. When reporter Marshall Kilduff tried to publish a story that did not portray the Peoples Temple in a positive light he was told it would not be published and he took his story to *New West* magazine. Many believe that the publication of the story, which included allegations by former Temple members about emotional, sexual, and physical abuse prompted to those remaining in the Temple to move to the Guyana compound.

"Jonestown"

The compound in Guyana was being built for several years prior to the publication of the article in the *New West*. It was built as a sanctuary and a socialist paradise from life in San Francisco. Guyana was chosen over Canada, Barbados, and Trinidad because of its socialist policies and it was a country with English as its native language. It was believed that the black leadership of the country would be more tolerant of the Temple and that the level of poverty in the country would allow Jones to more easily gain influence of the leaders. Jonestown was built in a communist model purposely, with Jones stating, "I believe we're the purest communists there are" Much like the communist countries of the Soviet Union, Cuba, and North Korea members were not allowed to leave Jonestown.

500 members of the Peoples Temple helped build Jonestown and in 1976 Guyana approved the lease it had negotiated in 1974. Jones negotiated an agreement with the Guyanese government that allowed Temple members mass migration to the country by stating that they were "skilled and progressive" and claimed that he had at least half a million dollars to invest in the small country. In 1976, Michael Propes, a member of the Peoples Temple asked Prime Minister Burnham to treat Jones as a "foreign dignitary along with other 'high ranking U.S. Officials'".

Jones travelled with California Lieutenant Governor Dymally and met with Prime Minister Burnham and the Minister of Foreign Affairs Fred Willis. During the meeting Dymally agreed that he would deliver a letter to the State Department stating that Guyana was open to cooperating with the United States. Later Dymally sent a letter to Burnham which touted Jones as "one of the finest human beings" Temple members were also encouraged to be loyal to Burnham's Peoples National Congress Party. One member of the Peoples Temple was even sexually involved with Guyana's ambassador to the United States.

In 1977, after the media reports in San Francisco from *New West* magazine, Jones and a few hundred members of the Peoples Temple relocated to Jonestown to escape the media scrutiny. This move made the population at Jonestown just under 1,000 people in 1978.

Although Temple members believed that Guyana would be a paradise on Earth, the arrival of Jones changed life significantly for those at Jonestown. Movies were not allowed anymore and Soviet propaganda was broadcast. Buildings became uninhabitable and school studies and lectures now became time for Jones to discuss revolution and enemies, Soviet alliances, and those who had defected from the Temple. Members worked six days a week, 12 hours a day followed by activities in a public pavilion. A system that Jones modeled on the North Korean system of eight hours of daily work and then eight hours of study. Children were not permitted to see their parents during the day. Jones began to refer to the U.S. as an evil capitalist country while praising Kim II-Sung, Robert Mugabe, and Joseph Stalin.

The only means of communication with the world outside of Jonestown was a shortwave radio. The FCC cited the Temple for violations and for using amateur frequencies for commercial purposes and threatened to revoke the license which would effectively end Jonestown's existence. The compound was on poor soil and was unable to grow food for the members so they had to import large amounts of wheat. Members, 45% of whom were black women, lived in community housing, eating meals of rice, beans, and greens with the occasional serving of meat or eggs. Jones, meanwhile, had his own small house with a refrigerator and often had eggs, meat, fruit, salad, and soft drinks. The lack of food combined with the poor hygiene caused an outbreak of severe diarrhea and high fevers in February 1978.

There was no prison and no formal form of capital punishment, but those who were considered to have serious disciplinary problems were punished in various forms. Those who were not seen a contributing enough to the community were given the job of cleaning the latrines or other heavy labor. Worse offenders were imprisoned in a 6 x 4 x 3-foot box and children were forced to spend the night at the bottom of a well, sometimes upside-down. Those who attempted to escape were drugged by Thorazine, sodium pentathol, Demerol, Valium or other sedative drugs and kept in an extended medical care area. Children were cared for communally and all members called Jones "Father" or "Dad."

Jones had begun showing his paranoia by speaking to members regarding their safety at Jonestown, going as far as to say that the CIA and other U.S. agencies were conspiring to destroy Jonestown and the members. When these "emergency situations" came about Jones would give the members four choices: try to get to the Soviet Union, flee into the jungle, commit "revolutionary suicide," or stay and fight the attackers. These nights were known a "White Nights" and on at least two occasions there was a simulated mass suicide. The Temple had been receiving shipments of ½ pounds of cyanide every month since 1976, under the guise of using it to clean gold. In May of 1978, the temple doctor wrote a memo asking Jones for permission to test the cyanide on the pigs at Jonestown.

The "Six Day Siege" and the Fight for Custody of John Stoen

In September of 1977, Tim and Grace Stoen, former members of the Peoples Temple fought in a Georgetown (the capital of Guyana) courthouse for custody of their five-year-old son, John, who was living in Guyana at Jonestown. After a few days, an order was issued for John to be taken into custody by Guyanese authorities. Jones refused to release the boy and the court issued an arrest for Jones himself. Jones was scared of being held in contempt of the courts orders so he concocted a fake sniper attack and the "White Nights" began, called the "Six Day Siege."

During these days, Jones warned members of the Temple about attacks from outsiders and Jonestown was surrounded by Peoples Temple Members with weapons such as machetes and guns. During the rallies, black activists like Angela Davis and Huey Newton were on the radio urging the members to stand strong against their enemies (of which there were none.) Jones proclaimed that they "would die unless they were granted freedom from harassment and asylum."

It took the Deputy Minister of Guyana to persuade Jones' wife, Marceline, that the Guyana Defence Forces were not planning on invading Jonestown. The Guyana clerk refused to sign the arrest warrant for Jones and it was obvious that his government connections had helped him again.

Jones now distrusted the Guyanese government and directed the members of the Temple to write foreign governments regarding their immigration. Jones himself wrote the U.S. State Department asking about the countries of North Korea and Albania. Members of the Peoples Temple in Georgetown were meeting with the embassies of the Soviet Union, North Korea, Yugoslovia, and Cuba. In October of 1978, a Soviet dignitary Feodor Timofeyez visited Jonestown and spoke to the members, saying in part "the Soviet Union would like to send our deepest and most sincere greetings to the people of this first socialist and communist community of the United States of America, in Guyana and in the world."

Members met with Timofeyev often to discuss relocating to the Soviet Union.

Members of the "Concerned Relatives" get involved

While all of this was happening in Guyana, in late 1977 and early 1978, Tim and Grace Stoen were meeting with other relatives of Jonestown residents, calling their informal group the "Concerned Relatives." Tim Stoen wrote letters to the U.S. Secretary of State and the Guyanese government. In January of 1978, he wrote to Congress and requested that individual congressman write to Prime Minister Burnham. Congressman Leo Ryan was one who wrote such a letter.

On February 17, 1978, Jones was interviewed by a reporter from the *San Francisco Examiner* in which Jones was questioned about the Stoen custody battle. The Peoples Temple threatened a lawsuit but the damage was done and the few who still supported Jones began to question his motives. Although Harvey Milk remained a supporter and wrote a letter to President Jimmy Carter calling Hones "a man of the highest character" and that those who had defected from the Temple were trying to "damage Jones' reputation with apparent bold-faced lies."

More letters were written by members of the "Concerned Relatives" and in June of 1978 Tim Stoen represented three members in lawsuits against Jones and other members of the Temple seeking over $56 million in damages. The attorney for the Peoples Temple, Charles R. Garry, filed a suit against Stoen seeking over $150 million in damages. Jones went further and enlisted the services of Mark Lane and Donald Freed, conspiracy theorists on the Kennedy assassination, to try and elevate the case against him and the Temple. Lane held press conferences which named the CIA, FBI, and the U.S. Post Office has having a conspiracy against the Temple. Although Lane presented himself as an uninterested party, Jones was paying him around $6,000 monthly to make these outrageous claims.

In 1978, Jones was diagnosed with a possible lung infection, although he announced to followers that he had lung cancer. The rumors were that he was abusing drugs and injected Valium, Quaaludes, LSD, stimulants, etc. and tapes from that time support the notion of Jones being in poor health. His medical problems included high blood pressure,

TIAs, rapid weight loss, convulsions, and temporary blindness. By November of 1978, Jones was experiencing enormous swelling of the extremities. While he was once a charismatic and appealing speaker, he now had problems finishing his sentences.

Congressman Leo Ryan goes to Jamestown

Congressman Leo Ryan, representing the 11th congressional district of California and a friend of Sammy Houston, was interested by the allegations made by the Concerned Relatives and agreed to visit Jonestown himself. On November 14th, Ryan and eighteen other people flew to Jonestown.

Initially the lawyers for Jones and the Peoples Temple, Lane and Garry, would not allow Ryan and his group access to Jonestown. Later they told Ryan that an airplane would take them to Port Kaituma, six miles from Jonestown, but due to seating restrictions on the aircraft only four members of the Concerned Relatives were allowed. At first only Ryan and three other members of the group were allowed inside Jonestown, although the rest were allowed in to the compound after sunset. The afternoon was spent listening to Jones talk to members about government conspiracies, all of which had been rehearsed prior to Ryan's arrival to convince the delegation that everyone was happy and healthy.

Later that night, Temple members Monica Bagby and Vernon Gosney saw Congressman Ryan's arrival as a route to an escape. But they mistook NBC reporter Harris for Ryan and passed him a note asking for his aid in helping them to defect. While Ryan, Speier, Dwyer, and Annibourne were invited to stay the night in Jonestown, other members of the delegation, including the press and members of Concerned Relatives, were forced to stay elsewhere.

The next morning, November 18th, eleven Temple members took a train to the town of Matthew's Ridge, in the opposite direction of Port Kaituma airstrip. This included the members of Jonestown's head of security, Joe Wilson. Later that day members of the Concerned Relatives group arrived at Jonestown and Marceline Jones gave them a tour. With the Congressmen's party at Jonestown, the Parks family, the Bogue families, Christopher O'Neal, and Harold Cordell asked to be escorted out of Jamestown with the Ryan delegation. Johnny, Jones' adopted son (Stoen?) tried to convince Jerry Parks from leaving, but Parks replied, "No way, it's nothing but a communist prison camp."

Jones gave his permission for the Parks, Bogue, O'Neal, and Cordell families, as well as Gosney and Bagby, to leave the camp. Harris showed Jones the note that had been handed to him by Gosney and Jones said that the defectors were lying and trying to destroy Jonestown.

There was an emotional standoff between families as well as within families regarding those wanting to leave and those wanting to stay. Al Simon, a Native American Temple member, wanted to take two of his children to Ryan so that the paperwork could be completed to take the children back to America. When Al's wife, Bonnie, was summoned over the loudspeakers by the Temple staff, she complained about her husband's decision and refused to leave.

The Massacre at Port Kaituma Airstrip

While most of the Ryan delegation arrived at the Port Kaituma airstrip in a large dump truck, Ryan and Dwyer stayed behind to handle the paperwork of any last-minute defectors. As the truck was leaving, Temple loyalist Larry Layton joined the group. Some of the defectors were concerned about Layton's decision and voiced their concerns/objections, but Layton was taken at his word and joined the group of those who wanted to leave Jonestown.

As the truck of people left Jonestown, a member of the Temple named Don "Ujara" Sly pulled a knife on Congressman Ryan. Ryan was not injured and Sly was wrestled to the ground. Dwyer told the Congressman to leave and he would file a criminal complaint against Sly. The truck carrying the passengers had turned around due to the attack on Ryan and he joined them to go to Port Kaituma.

Originally, they had chartered a 19-passenger plane from Guyana Airways to fly them back to the capital city. The number of defectors required them to need another six-passenger Cessna. The delegation was supposed to leave around 4:45 but the planes were not yet there and they had to wait until 5:10 for the planes to arrive. Layton, the last of the defectors, was on the Cessna. As the plane taxied to the end of the airstrip he pulled a gun and began shooting. Bagby and Gosney were injured while Dale Parks took the gun away from him.

Some passengers had gotten on the larger plane when the Temple's security squad pulled up in a tractor trailer. When the tractor was about 30 feet away from the plane, at almost the same time that Layton began shooting on the smaller plane, the security team opened fire from the tractor with at least two shooters circling the plane on foot.

There were around nine shooters, but their identities are still uncertain, although most agree that Joe Wilson, Thomas Kice, Sr., and Ronnie Dennis were three of them. NBC cameraman Bob Brown had his videotape rolling when the shooting began and Brown, Robinson, Harris, and defector Patricia Parks were shot in the first few minutes. Congressman Ryan was shot more than 20 times and nine people were left injured, including Speier, Sung, Dwyer, Reiterman, and Anthony Katsaris.

The pilots of the two planes got into the Cessna to fly to Georgetown while the damaged larger plane and the injured passengers were left on the airstrip.

Meanwhile in Jonestown

Before leaving Jonestown, Ryan had told attorney Garry that he would report positive things about the conditions at Jonestown to those back in the U.S. Ryan had interviewed 60 relatives and only 14 of over 900 of the Peoples Temple wanted to leave, a very small percentage. Garry told Jones this information, but Jones could not be convinced, saying "I have failed" and "all is lost."

There is a 44-minute tape, known as the "death tape," which records part of the meeting that Jones called that evening. Prior to the meeting his aides had prepared the deadly concoction that would end in mass suicide. Unlike the reports and stories have led us to believe, it was not Kool-Aid, but rather grape flavored Flavor Aid mixed with Valium, chloral hydrate, cyanide, and Phenergan (Phenergan is a medication which acts as an anti-emetic, meaning it helped the people not vomit the poisonous mixture.) On the tape, Jones told the group that there would be a shooting at one of the planes, the plane would crash into the jungle and people would be parachuting into the jungle so there had better not be any children left. "The ones that they take captured, they're gonna just let them grow up and be dummies."

There were discussions among Temple members about a possible airlift to the USSR rather than revolutionary suicide; however, after the shooters returned Jones informed the group that Congressman Ryan had been murdered at which point some members praised Jones and the choice to commit suicide.

Flavor-Aid

The first member to take the poisonous concoction were Ruletta Paul and her one-year-old infant. They used a syringe to squirt it into the babies' mouth and then Paul squirted the poison into her own mouth. Survivor Stanley Clayton said that when adults began to see the poison take effect they were reluctant to take it themselves.

Death occurred within five minutes of taking the poison. After drinking, people were escorted down a walkway that led outside the pavilion. Jones urged the people, saying "Die with a degree of dignity. Lay down your life with dignity, don't lay down with tears and agony...I tell you. I don't care how many screams you hear, I don't care how many anguished cries...death is a million times preferable to 10 more days of this life. If you knew what was ahead of you – if you knew what was ahead of you, you'd be glad to be stepping over tonight."

While some survivors say that the people showed no panic and instead they acted almost trance-like, this is contradicted by the death tape on which you can hear children screaming and crying.

Jones' body was found next to his chair, his head resting on a pillow. The Guyanese Chief Medical Examiner reported that the cause of death was a gunshot wound to his left temple that was self-inflicted.

The Jonestown mass suicide was the greatest deliberate loss of American civilian lives until September 11, 2001.

The evening of November 18th, at the headquarters in Georgetown, Sharon Amos, a member of the Peoples Temple, got a radio communication from Jones which instructed those at the headquarters to take revenge on the enemies of the Temple and then commit revolutionary suicide. When the police arrived, Amos took her children, Liane, Christa, and Martin into a bathroom with a knife. Amos killed Christa, age 11, Martin, age 10, and the she and Liane, age 21, helped each other kill themselves with the knife.

Survivors

Three members of Jonestown who were high ranking in the Temple survived and claimed that they had been given an assignment which is why they did not die. Tim Carter, Mike Carter, and Mike Prokes had luggage with $550,000 U.S. dollars, $130,000 Guyanese dollars, and an envelope which they were instructed to take to the Soviet Embassy in the capital of Georgetown. Inside the envelope were two passports and three letters.

The letters listed accounts of over $7.3 million that was to be transferred to the Communist Party of the Soviet Union. The three men were caught as they were going to a boat belonging to the Temple that was at Kaituma. They could not have reached Georgetown, 150 miles away, as the boat had been sent away that day. They were given this final job before the suicides started but abandoned the plan when they realized what was happening. Tim Carter saw his son and wife taking the poison and had to be physically pulled from the scene by his brother.

Lawyers Garry and Lane had been taken to a house that was used for visitors before the suicide and went into the jungle to head toward Port Kaituma when they heard gunshots. Other survivors were: Clayton, who had hidden in the jungle; Rhodes, who volunteered to get a stethoscope and hid under a building; Grover Davis, who, at 79 and hearing impaired, did not hear the announcement and lay in a ditch pretending to be dead; and Hyacinth Thrash, aged 76, who crawled under her bed and hid.

The Guyanese Medical Examiner Mootoo was the only doctor to initially examine the scene. Mootoo visually examined over 200 bodies and later claimed that there were needle marks on at least 70 of the bodies (it is still unknown if those needle marks were for those who did not die quickly enough or if they were on people who refused to drink the Flavor-Aid mixture.) It was Mootoo and an American pathologist who informed the public that cyanide was found in some bodies while the remaining liquid had different tranquilizers, potassium chloride, and potassium cyanide.

There was a gunshot wound on the body of Annie Moore which Mootoo said could not have been self-inflicted (although she had also taken a lethal amount of cyanide.)

Letters left from the Deceased

A letter was found near the body of Marceline Jones which was typewritten and dated November 18, 1978, signed by Marceline and witnessed by Moore and Maria Katsaris which read that she would leave all of her bank assets to the Communist Party of the USSR. She would go on to describe Jonestown as being "the most peaceful, loving community that ever existed" and that everything written about Jim Jones were "lies."

After the Revolutionary Suicide

Reiterman photographed the aftermath of the shootings at the Port Kaituma. Dwyer was grazed by a bullet, and Layton was arrested by Guyanese authorities. Most of the survivors at the airstrip slept in the Port Kaituma café while those who were more seriously injured slept in a tent at the airstrip. Five teenage members of the Parks and Bogue families hid in the jungle and were lost for three days until the Guyanese soldiers found them. The Guyanese government sent an airplane the next day to evacuate those who were wounded.

` Rhodes arrived in Port Kaituma the night of November 18, 1978 and Clayton arrived there the next morning. Prokes and the Carter brothers were taken into protective custody and later released in Georgetown along with Rhodes, Clayton, Garry and Lane. Prokes would commit suicide in March of 1979.

Layton, who had started the shooting on the plane, was found not guilty of attempted murder in court in Guyana using the "not guilty by reason of insanity" defense. He was later tried in the U.S. under the federal statute of assassinating members of Congress and internationally protected people (meaning Congressman Ryan and Deputy Chief of Mission of the U.S. embassy to Guyana Dwyer). He was convicted in the U.S. of conspiracy as well as aiding and abetting the murder of Ryan and the attempted murder of Dwyer. Paroled in 2002, Layton is the only person to have been held criminally responsible or served jail/prison time for the events at Jonestown.

After the Jonestown deaths, the "Cult Awareness Network" was formed. They were involved with helping families get their loved ones out of groups such as:

"The Family International," "Scientology," and "The Branch Davidians. The group ceased to exist in 1996.

Four hundred of the bodies would be buried in a mass grave at the Evergreen Cemetery in Oakland, California.

The site in Guyana was first taken care of by the Guyanese government and held Hmong refugees from Laos for a time during the 1980. A fire destroyed many buildings during the 80s. The site was deserted as the jungle took over the remaining buildings and leftovers from the Jonestown Era. In 1998, Jim Jones, Jr., was taping a segment for the TV news program *20/20* and found the remains of an oil drum which he recognized as one that held some of the poison from the night in November of 1978.

In 2003, a television crew returned to the site for the 25th anniversary and looked for any remaining artifacts. The place of death of around 900 people had only a cassava mill, the remains of a tractor, a generator, a filing cabinet, an overturned truck, a fuel pump, a steel drum, and an organ.

Over 900 people died at Jonestown, as well as those at Port Kaituma and Georgetown, as a result of direct orders by Jim Jones. Others have died by suicide due to the events that occurred at Jonestown and under the oversight of the Revered Jones. Still others have had their lives touched, or altered, by the loss of life on the day in November of 1978. The power and influence that Jim Jones held and controlled is truly amazing. There are still websites today which portray these events in a different light, and others that see Jim Jones as a savior.

t."

"Eh, that's alright." Andre pushed himself up and took the jacket from her.

"Thanks for loaning it to me the other night, by the way."

"No problem." Andre waved goodbye and headed out the door. Ava followed and closed it behind him.

The next day she received a call from Charlie asking her to come down to the police station. Her stomach tossed and turned the whole way there. She hadn't really been able to eat too much since the night everything happened. Ava took a deep breath and trudged into the station. A few people stared at her as she walked in. Other avoided looking at her all together. She bit her lip and rapped her knuckles on the Chief's door.

"Yep, come in." He was shuffling through paperwork as she walked into his office. He glanced up at her, "Close the door behind you."

"What's going on, Chief?" Ava closed the door with a click behind her and sat across from Charlie.

"Well, Brooks, I wanted to be the first to tell you that the man you apprehended—Elan Parker—confessed to the murders of those four girls we found."

A sigh of relief exploded from Ava, "I *knew* it had to be him!"

"Hang on, I'm not done yet."

"Yes, sir. Sorry, sir." She tucked her hand into her lap and looked at the tops of her knees.

"Turns out that Parker attended the same church as Ridgway. Shared some of his same ideals. Once Ridgway was arrested, Parker took it on himself to," Charlie motioned with air quotes, "carry on the vision and rid the world of the unclean women." He mumbled under his breath, "Self-righteous prick."

"So what happens now?"

"Well, he's going to jail. D.A. is just battering around details of his sentence now. Trying to see if he can help find any other victims that Ridgway may not have revealed yet."

"Ok," Ava nodded determinedly. She felt as though she had made some progress towards proving herself.

"Parker isn't the only reason I wanted to talk to you today."

Ava's heart sank from the pain that crossed momentarily across the Chief's face. "What is it?" Apprehension filled her gut.

"You went directly against my orders in doing this, Ava. You put yourself and members of the public in danger because of your actions."

"I saved two girls' lives!" Ava pushed away from the desk and stood up.

"I know," he held his hands up defensively, "but that doesn't change the fact that you went against orders. I have to suspend you."

"Unbelievable! I helped you find a killer before he killed anyone else." She leaned down towards him. Her blood was boiling.

"Brooks, I'm going to have to ask you to watch your tone." Charlie stood up, towering above her.

Ava clenched her jaw and shook her head, "I can't believe this. How long is my suspension?"

"Two months."

"Two months! Are you kidding me?"

"During that time, I set up a place for you to volunteer at the Vine Maple Place. I think it might help you get in touch with your core beliefs a little better. You also have to see a psychologist to deal with any residual trauma from that night in the lumber mill, and honestly maybe some issues you're having still from the loss of your mother."

Vine Maple Place was an organization that helped families find their feet after hardships. It also helped kids that were on the path to living on the street. Kids that might one day end up like Steph if not for some extra help. Ava nodded and left his office in silence.

Maybe Charlie was right. Maybe this was what she needed right now. Volunteering there would give her a sense of accomplishment and the knowledge that she was making a difference in the lives of those families. It was more of an immediate spiritual reward than trailing a criminal from body to body and just hoping to stop them before someone else was killed. She knew she was meant to make a difference in the world. She had come too far to fall under the shadow of the heartache that men like Ridgway and Parker cast. She was determined to fight against the current.